Stop
MOURNING
—— Start ——
GROWING

DELSEA FLOWERS

STRATTON
—PRESS—
Publishing Life

Stop Mourning Start Growing
Copyright © 2021 **Delsea Flowers**

Stratton Press Publishing
831 N Tatnall Street Suite M #188,
Wilmington, DE 19801
www.stratton-press.com
1-888-323-7009

ISBN (Paperback): 978-1-64895-404-7
ISBN (Ebook): 978-1-64895-405-4

Printed in the United States of America

This is a story of falling down a ladder and climbing back up with two broken legs as they heal. You can't imagine how far you can go until your faith has been tested. So the fight of a battle to get out of that dark shadow has begun. Words of encouragement to fight off that angry beast called pain. Do something outside of yourself that's fun and exciting to keep you busy until it fades away. The strength within the power will win. Allow your soul to strive and give in and cry. It's good to break down, but never stay down. Let it out, shout it out, exhale! When talking becomes more than it bears that people no longer want to hear, to silence yourself will keep the pain locked in. This is when paper and pen become your best friend.

Chapter

ONE

Dana worked in one of the roughest jails in New York. She was five feet tall, with a caramel chocolate complexion and short curly hair. She was in her thirties. She was a mean and strong corrections officer.

On a very cold night, Dana sat there freezing, shaking like a leaf on a cold plastic chair. Every night working on that cold post was hard. There was no heat, with a door directly on her back and a door in front of her. She was getting sicker and sicker as the nights went by. Her cold got worst. Even with all the hot tea and lemon she drank, she still lost her voice.

Dana mounted her feet on a milk crate to keep the mice from running up her legs as they searched for heat and food.

Early in the morning, Dana called out the names of the inmates who had to get ready for court. One rudely yelled back at her, "You go, CO!"

She angrily yelled back, "After you!" and turned on all of the lights.

All the other inmates woke up, yelling, "Turn off the lights!"

She yelled back, "After all the court inmates are up and ready to go!"

One inmate, who was six feet seven inches and weighing 310 lb., got up and yelled, "Man, you must be crazy. I got to go back to work in a few hours. Get your ass up and get the hell out of here before I hurt somebody!"

The court inmates jump out of their beds and into the showers with fear that he will hurt one of them.

Dana smiled and kindly turned the lights out, almost forgetting about the cold and the mice running around her feet.

* * *

On January 20, Dana went on vacation. She spent most of the time working on that cold, and it got a little better. By the time she returned to work, she got sick again. This time she called in sick and went to see her doctor. He told her she had an upper respiratory infection. He prescribed her some antibiotics and Claritin. She took seven antibiotics and three Claritin when she discovered her period was late. Dana was afraid to continue taking the medicine, so she took an EPT test. The results came up positive.

Dana then made an appointment to see her OB-GYN to find out definitely. Just in case the EPT was wrong. All she could think about was why now, after losing all that weight, all that hard working out. What would Chase say? She knew exactly what he would say: "Let's go out and celebrate." He would not think twice about all the hard work Dana did to lose her weight. Six months of discipline and starvation.

Chase was a tall dark handsome family man, standing five feet and nine inches, with a coco chocolate complexion. He was slim and handsome, as well as responsible and strong minded. He had to be to handle a mean little woman like Dana. She was five feet two inches, caramel complexion, and sexy. Chase had really been good for Dana. Her whole attitude had changed; she became a nicer person. Dana's daughter Tina noticed that her mother was not so mean anymore. She would always comment, "Mommy, I'm so glad you're not as mean like you used to be." Dana never noticed she was that mean. She blamed it on lack of sleep.

Dana walked in the doctor's office where a slangy short woman sat behind the desk. She had curly black hair and couldn't merely speak English. She ran her finger up and down the schedule until she found Dana's name. "Mrs. Frazier, your appointment is at 12:45. You have about six people in the head of you."

Dana grunted, "Six?"

"Please have seat, he'll be with you soon."

Dana walked over to a brown-and-black chair. She took a seat next to an elderly lady with a cane, who was waiting for her ride to pick her up. "The car is not here yet?" she yelled to the male aide.

The aide was standing by the door, opening it to look out. "No, not yet, I will let you know."

As Dana sat there, her mind began to wander. How did she get there again? Wow! Pregnant! This would be her third child. She promised to give Chase two children. Plus Tina, she's not Chase. Three was the cutoff for children. Tina was sixteen, five feet and an inch tall, with skin the color of caramel chocolate. She was a little bit chubby, but very cute. Zeek was a typical three-year-old—cute, loud, and active.

When did this all start? Back in Boston was where it all began. Dana went to visit her cousin Pam. Pam was five feet and seven inches tall. She was a slim woman in her early thirties with dark brown skin and short-cut hair. They were sitting in the room watching TV and talking. They were deciding on what to have for dinner. They decided to have pizza. Pam said, "Let me comb my hair." Dana had her hair wrapped up with bobby pins in it. She didn't want to comb it out. So she put a scarf on her head and said, "I'm not combing my hair out, give me a hat. Nobody out here knows me." Pam gave her a purple hat. Dana looked at it and said, "A purple hat, but I got on red glasses." They laughed! Dana yelled, "Oh, what the heck, nobody knows me out here!"

Walking to the restaurant, Dana noticed two men were sitting in the restaurant. "Oh no, Pam!" Dana yelled. "There are men in there!"

"Oh well, I combed my hair." Pam laughed and said, "You never know who you might meet when you look your worse."

Dana's heart beat with fear. She took a deep breath as they walked in the restaurant. Heading straight to the counter to order, Dana decided not to look back for anything. They placed the order. Then one guy tapped Pam on her back and said, "Aren't you Pam, Larry's cousin?"

Pam responded, "Oh yeah, you're Chase. You helped him move me that day."

They began talking, and Pam walked over to his table. Dana stayed at the counter until the cook asked if he can help her with something else. Dana said no and went to sit at a table across from them.

Chase told Pam that he worked as a corrections officer for Suffolk County. Dana heard Pam say, "Oh yeah? My cousin is a corrections officer in New York."

He turned and looked at Dana with the biggest smile ever. Dana wanted to crawl under the table. "So you work in corrections?" he asked.

Dana cleared her throat and took a deep breath. Then she replied yes.

"Tell me, how is it?"

Dana didn't know where to begin; she couldn't even remember at that point. All she wanted to do was take off that purple hat and red glasses and comb her hair down. "It's okay, gets a little tough sometimes."

The cook suddenly yelled out, "One large extra cheese pizza!"

Dana jumped up to grab the pizza and go. They all said goodbye. Dana whispered to Pam, "He is fine! Invite them to the house."

Pam replied, "You invite them."

Dana argued, "I don't know them, you do."

"Don't worry, I'll call Larry. He can get in touch with him for you."

Larry was a mutual friend of Chase and Pam. He was five feet and six inches, with dark skin and was quite skinny. He was in his late thirties.

The call to Larry was unsuccessful. He didn't have Chase's number but said he would go to his mother's house to find out where he lived.

Two days later, Larry came by and said he hadn't gone to Chase's mother's house yet. Dana yelled, "Well, let's go over there now!"

Pam and Larry looked at each other, and both agreed to go. They took three buses and a train to where Larry thought Chase's mother still lived. However, she no longer lived there.

Dana was heartbroken. She wanted to find Chase even more. They continued to search around the area she first met him. Before long, her vacation was over.

Six months later, Dana returned to Boston on vacation again. On Friday they went out to a club. On Saturday they went to the hair salon. By the time they returned to the house, there was a message on the machine from Larry that said, "This message is for Dana. Chase's number is…"

Pam ran to get a pen and wrote down the number.

Dana jumped up and yelled, "Oh yes! Yes!"

Pam picked up the phone quickly and dialed Chase's number. She spoke to him a few minutes and then passed the phone to Dana. Dana's heart dropped; she didn't know what to say. All this time looking for him, this man she craved for over six months. She was now speechless.

She took the phone slowly and said, "Hello?"

Chase responded back with, "Hello, would you like to go for a ride?" Dana smiled and hit Pam in the arm as she answered, "Sure."

"Okay, I'll pick you up in twenty-five minutes."

She hung up, and she and Pam do a victory dance. Dana made sure everything was right and tight this time.

When the doorbell rang, her heart began to race.

Once in the car, Chase began to speak before he even pulled off. He said, "I want to let you know that I'm living with someone."

Dana's heart dropped as she continued to listen.

"It's not working out. When the lease is up in four months, I will be moving out. We're in separate rooms. Are you okay with that?"

Dana respected his honesty. Not many men would be so honest. "Sure, if it's okay with you."

He drove off, and they soon arrived at the boardwalk, where they took a stroll. There was a lot of talk about his and her job. They both fell head over heels in love.

About a year later, Zeek was born. The day of their first anniversary, they signed the contract for their new home. Months after they married, Zeek was four months and Tina was fourteen years old.

* * *

"Mrs. Frazier! Mrs. Frazier!"

Dana is awakened out of her daydreaming of her past.

"Mrs. Frazier!"

"Yes?"

"The doctor will see you now."

11

"You are definitely pregnant, at least eight weeks," the doctor said, smiling. "Congratulations!"

Dana was a little depressed. She had just lost forty pounds, and she looked and felt great. She was worried about swelling up and getting big again. Dana was not sure she's ready to do it again. Chase would never agree to an abortion.

Once she got home, she walked into the kitchen to Chase and said, "I'm pregnant, and I'm not keeping it."

He said, "Okay" and said nothing else. He drove her to the clinic. When they arrived, he still said nothing. He wanted to see the forms. And then he walked away with tears in his eyes.

Dana walked back to the waiting room, but Chase didn't accompany her. Dana sat there looking around at everyone there. She suddenly realized what she was about to do. She thought that she was not doing anything wrong by having another baby. She was married to a beautiful man and had two lovely children.

She jumped up, went to the desk, and said, "I'm leaving. I don't belong here." She hurriedly walked out without looking back. She got in the car, and Chase looked at her. Dana said, "I changed my mind."

"I didn't understand why we was here in the first place," he argued. "We both have good jobs, we have a nice home with extra rooms. I know I'm not home yet, but as soon as I get a good job in New York, I be home. I do my best to try to take care of my family."

Dana said, "I know, it's not you, it was me worrying about gaining my weight back, that's all. Just being selfish.

Let's go home and take the kids out for breakfast and tell them the good news."

After Dana told the kids the news, Tina said, "Whatever you have, Mom, please have a girl. Not another boy."

Zeek said, "No, a boy."

"Sorry, Zeek, but that's a girl, I know it," Chase said.

Dana told the good news to her good friend Myra. A couple days later, Myra brought the baby its first gift. Wrapped in a nice gift box was a pretty white sweater with matching hat and cute little shoes. It was so unexpected since Dana was only eight weeks pregnant. Myra said she was in the process of getting her house, so she thought she would give her something now. She joked, "Besides, I might not be able to afford it later. Think of it as getting you ready for the little one, whether it's a boy or girl."

Dana felt so special. She hugged her and thanked her so much. Myra was the first one on the job to know Dana was expecting. Myra had a Spanish accent, and she was about five feet and 150 lb. Myra and Dana were both trying to lose weight to get to 130 lb. Dana did make her goal, at least, before she would gain it back again.

Chase still commuted back and forth from Boston to New York. He was so happy to be a father again. He was so supportive and did everything for his family in the little time he spent home.

Whenever Chase was away, Dana's sister Cindy would stay with her to help her out. Chase would come home faithfully every Sunday morning straight from work. He would go back on Tuesday night to go straight to work.

Dana really enjoyed his company when he was home. Chase and Dana's sister Cindy got along great. He would tell her about all the crazy stories that happened with him and Dana, and she would tell him about their crazy childhood. One of his favorites was sitting in the car, waiting for Dana to get in. When she did sit in the car, she sat on a bee. Dana jumped up and started screaming and sprang her back side up from the seat. A bee flew up past Chase and went out the window. Chase yelled, "That was a bee! He must have stung you!"

Dana started screaming and jumped out of the car and ran to the house. She didn't have time to get the key out, and she started unzipping her pants. Dana ran to the door, ringing the doorbell, yelling, "Open the door!"

Tina opened the door. Dana pulled her pants down and ran to the chair with her butt in the air, yelling, "Get it out!"

Chase came in behind her and shook his head. He then walked to the bathroom to get a pair of tweezers to search for the stinger.

Dana yelled, "Close the curtain!"

As Chase told the story, Cindy laughed till she had tears in her eyes.

Most people thought Cindy and Dana were twins. Cindy was shorter at exactly five feet, with fair skin and long straight hair. They both wore their hair alike most times. Cindy had a nice shape. Dana and Cindy were the closest sisters out of six.

Cindy told Chase her famous story about family fights. They came from a very large family. You can't imagine the fights they had with each other or out in the streets.

Dana and Cindy would always double team whoever they fought. One sister named Acee used to always run away and leave them. They called her Acee because she liked to play cards. Tina and Zeek thought Acee looked a lot like a famous female rapper.

Chase's family wasn't so big. His mother and father both died when he was very young. His mother was murdered, stabbed in the street on her way home one night. He hardly remembers her. When he was thirteen, his father passed away from throat cancer, which stopped him from ever smoking. He had about five brothers and three sisters. His foster mother raised him from age thirteen. His father did what he could do before he passed away. Whatever happened in his past made him the man that he is today—a family oriented, honest, content, hardworking, and a handsome man. Tina was not Chase's real daughter, but he was just like a real dad to her.

One day when Dana was at work, she was scheduled to work the A station that they called the bubble. One officer would be inside an office with two housing areas on the outside of the station. The other officer would walk from one side to the other side to tour the areas.

Dana was very concerned about working in that situation. If a fight broke out on either side, it could cause her blood pressure to rise. There were a total of one hundred inmates, fifty on each side. Dana was very concerned for both of their safety. She was not supposed to leave the station for any reason but hit her alarm for the pro team to come.

Guess exactly what happened. While the officer was touring one side, on the other side, a fight broke out.

Dana screamed, "Break it up!" while she had to get the officer from one side to the other side to control the situation. She hit her alarm for backup, just in case it was a setup to take over the jail.

Right after that incident, Dana refused to work around inmates anymore while she was pregnant. They continued to schedule her on one, but she always informed the captain that if she worked that post, he would be responsible if anything should happen. After that, they changed her post to somewhere safe.

* * *

Zeek was going to have a hard time adjusting to the new baby. Dana is seven months now, and she already gained 40 lb. She was as big as a house. Thank god she already passed the worst part, which was soreness of her breasts, that made her cry from the pain. The nausea and tiredness from the hot summer heat was unbearable. She would drink so much ice water, she felt like she would burst.

Dana was home from work on maternity leave. Finally October, it's almost over. Dana's cousin Pam was hoping she had the baby on her birthday, October 23, as a birthday present.

Well, on October 22, Dana went to the bathroom. There was a big gush of fluid. Dana called her doctor. He told her if she felt any pain or contractions coming close, call him and go to the hospital.

Dana called Chase in Boston. She said, "Come home immediately, I'm going into labor." Chase arrived home about 10:00 p.m. Dana remained home until 3:00

a.m. She went upstairs to tell Tina they were going to the hospital. Dana prepared Zeek's clothes for Tina to take him next door to the neighbor when she had to go to school. Tina knew exactly what do.

Chapter

TWO

Dana was in the hospital single room, hooked on a monitor for the baby's heartbeat. Chase sat in a chair falling off and on to sleep. He would wake up every time Dana had a contraction. Dana was so tired, she was falling off and on sleep herself. Dana was having weird dreams with thick white clouds and an angel flying by, waving. She was suddenly awakened by another contraction.

It was now 7:00 a.m., and Dr. Alex arrived. After he examined Dana, he noticed that the baby had not dropped into Dana's pelvis yet.

He had another doctor come in to examine Dana for a second opinion. They wanted to have a C-section to make sure the baby made it out safely without the cord wrapping around the baby's neck. Dana was worried about getting that needle in her back. She prayed her contraction would not make her move from the pain. Her heart was pounding; she was about to give birth to her baby girl. Dana and Chase knew it was a girl when she had an amniocentesis.

The room was so cold, Dana couldn't feel anything from her breasts down. She trembled, but only the upper body would shake. Chase was right by her side. Dana told Chase she felt a knife cutting down her stomach.

The anesthesiologist heard her and said, "What? You feel the cutting?"

She replied, "I feel it, but it doesn't hurt. It feels like a finger marking it."

The anesthesiologist put more drugs in the IV to make sure Dana didn't feel the pain. Then Dana felt the doctor pulling the baby out of her stomach. Her body was like dead weight; she could not move, only her head. She turned to look at Chase to see how he was holding on. He was fine with a big smile of excitement, just like when they had Zeek. They had a blue cover over Dana, so he couldn't see everything.

Dana looked at the doctor as he said, "Oh, there she is. Wow, she's a big baby, nine pounds!"

Dana heard her cry. After they cleaned her up, the nurse put the baby in Chase's arms. He was smiling, looking down at her.

Dana yelled, "Can I see her for a second?"

Chase forgot all about her. He brought Armani to her and apologized. She had a beautiful fat face with curly hair. Dana started to cry. She wanted to hold her, but she couldn't as her arms were strapped down to the IV blood pressure machine.

The nurse came and took Armani to put her in the incubator with a little hat on her head. As they continued to sew her up, Dana joked with the doctor, "Don't forget to tie my tubes. This is it."

He joked back and said, "Oh no, I think we forgot the female side."

Dana yelled, "You better not!"

Chase came over and kissed Dana and said, "Well, that's over now. It's time for the healing time."

Dana put her head back and exhaled, thinking of the moment when the drugs would wear off.

* * *

Chase brought the kids to the hospital to see Dana and the baby. Zeek was a little confused, but when he saw his little sister, he felt like a big brother. "That's my baby sister," he said with a little smirk on his face. No matter what happened, he demanded more attention.

Dana spent all day to late night with Armani. They bonded. There was no way they could have given her the wrong baby. Armani was the biggest baby in the nursery. The neighbor next door, Wilma, came to visit. She joked about how big Armani's head and chest were in the nursery. Armani was much bigger than the other babies. Zeek was 6 lb. 10 oz., and Tina was 6 lb. 4 oz. Dana had gained seventy pounds during pregnancy. She was 200 lb. during birth.

It was the fifth day Dana was in the hospital. Dana had been discharged to leave. The pediatrician had come to discharge the baby. He said as he examined her, "I want her to see a pediatric cardiologist. I hear a little heart murmur."

Dana looked at him as her heart drop.

He continued, "I want to make sure that it is one that will close on its own."

There was no way Dana was leaving without her baby, so she and Chase waited all day. They were sitting in the chair in the hospital, waiting for the pediatric cardiologist to come to examine Armani. Dana was talking to Chase when all of a sudden, she felt a knocking in the middle of her spine. It shook her. Again and again, repeatedly, it didn't stop. It felt like her back was closing in.

Chase jumped up to get the nurse.

Dana grabbed his hand, yelling, "Don't leave me!" She was so afraid; she had no idea what was going on. She needed him to get help, but she couldn't let his hand go. She bounced up and down in the chair, sliding toward the floor. Finally Chase yelled to the nurse, "My wife needs help!"

The nurse ran in, and Dana yelled, "Get Dr. Chuo!"

The nurse ran out immediately to get Dr. Chuo, who was the doctor who gave Dana the spinal tap. She ran back in and said the doctor was in the middle of a procedure. The knocking slowed down, then somehow it stopped. Dana gained control to sit up without the knocking. The doctor came in to see Dana. Chase described what happen. The doctor claimed it must have been a muscle spasm.

Finally the nurse came in and took the baby and said, "The doctor is here."

Dana and Chase waited about two hours while they were in the nursery with the lights off. No one ever said anything to them. The nurse finally brought the baby back in the room. She said, "The doctor will be here to talk to you after I get her papers together." She left, and then she returned to take the baby again and said, "We need to check her oxygen level."

This time when she brought the baby back in, the doctor came in with her. She didn't introduce herself; she just started to speak. "Okay, Dr. Frank said she has a small hole, what I see is a huge hole. Her pulmonary valves are pumping very slow, it's like her heart is on the wrong side or something." She began to draw a picture on a piece of paper to describe what she was saying. Then she said she would not release Armani unless they promise to bring her to see her on Friday. She continued to say that she started to call an ambulance and have her rush to the hospital.

Chase and Dana looked at each other. Chase said, "Well then, do that. We don't want to risk taking her home and risking her life."

Dr. Steven said, "Well, if we keep her in the hospital, all we're going to do is watch, feed, and change her. That's what you would do at home. She could be there for months. Just watch her and make sure that her mouth doesn't turn blue. If anything happens, you can call me."

"Can we rush her to the hospital in our area?" Dana asked.

Dr. Steven responded, "You can rush her there. I mean, it's not like she's a car with a flat tire, and you can just hand her to us and say to fix her. I know you think you have a healthy baby, but you don't. She's a sickly baby, and you just have to handle that."

Chase and Dana were both thinking, *This can't be happening. How can this lady be so heartless?*

When they left the hospital, Dana's heart was so broken. Dana was in so much pain and stress knowing something was wrong with her baby's heart. Chase had to go back to Boston that night for work. The next morning, Chase had to return to New York. Pam came over to help Dana while he was away.

Dana was suffering from so much pain in the back of her neck and head. She couldn't even look down at Armani to put a bottle in her mouth. Dana was so glad when they walked in the door. Dana was against the wall with Armani in her arms. Dana was holding Armani as high as she could to hold the bottle in her mouth. Pam came in and took the baby. Chase dropped the bags and helped Dana to a chair.

Pam was one of Dana's most reliable people in the world. She is very free-hearted, caring person. Pam will help out anyone who needs help. Pam is a very hyper energetic person. She's a busy, fun, and exciting person. Pam's average height is about five feet and seven inches tall. She was very slim toward the top, but toward the bottom, she carried a truckload, as Dana would say. Pam had dark skin with a cute short haircut that she kept looking good.

Chase went food shopping. They both had to convince Dana to eat something. Pam gave Dana some Motrin, which stopped the pain for a while. They discussed taking Armani to another doctor for a second opinion. Dana called the pediatrician to recommend someone else. He recommended Dr. Boxx to her. Dana made an appointment to see him the next morning. Pam had to drive while Dana was still taking painkillers. Pam had to make sure Dana would eat before taking the pills.

Once they arrived at the hospital, they met the staff. They were all very nice except the receptionist; she was very nasty. Dr. Boxx was so sweet and kind. He reminded Pam and Dana of the dad in *Honey, I Shrunk the Kids*. He came in with his shoes off. He was so kind, he made Dana feel like Armani was in safe hands. He used a pediatric cardiograph for the baby. Dr. Steven used an adult cardiograph because that was all they had available in the hospital. Dana hoped it would make a difference.

Dr. Boxx said Armani had two holes in her heart. There was a hole in the upper chamber and one in the lower chamber. He said that her valves were thicker than they were supposed to be. "The blood is pumping kind of slow. Take her home, and treat her like a normal baby. As long as she's drinking and gaining weight, that's what we want." He would see her again in a month's time. He was very pleasant. He was glad to see Pam was with Dana for support. He was surprised to hear that Armani's father was a correction officer in Boston. He shouted, "Wow! I better be careful, or he will arrest me." His eyes almost popped out when he found out that Dana was one too. He was extremely funny and pleasant. He made them feel real comfortable receiving the bad news.

Dana was still upset by the news, but for some strange reason, the pain in her head and neck went away.

Dr. Boxx was very nice. He stood about five feet four inches tall, pale skin, with glasses. He spoke softly as he pushed his glasses up with his finger. Dr. Boxx gave Dana lots of hope. He showed Dana and Pam pictures of children with similar conditions as Armani who were now age five or seven years old. He also decided to do a second echocardiogram of his own.

When the echocardiogram was performed, Pam and Dana stayed in the room the whole time they were examining her. Dana held her little hands and talked to Armani the whole time to keep her still. So they were able to hook up the EKG wires to the right area. They were all nice and understanding and sensible to the baby's condition, except the receptionist who walked in on the middle of the test. She was complaining about the phone number Dana gave her to the insurance company. The technician yelled at her, "Can you close the door? You can take care of that when I'm finished!"

Chapter

THREE

D ana and Chase were told not to let Armani get a cold when they left the hospital. Dana had everything mapped down. Whenever Zeek, Tina, Chase, or Dana got home, they had to take off all their clothes and wash up and change. Then they can come around the baby. They all kept that up, but then Armani began to get cradle cap, and it was hard to get out.

Dana didn't want to wash her hair too much because she was afraid of her getting a cold on cool days. So Dana used baby oil and brushed it out softly to keep her from getting sick. Sometimes Dana would stare into Armani's eyes; it felt like she was trying to tell her something. Like, "Mommy, what is going on with my little body?" Dana would stare so hard into her eyes that see would notice a tiny white dot in the center of her pupil. It looked like a tiny star in her right eye.

When Dana took Armani for her two-week checkup with her pediatrician Dr. Frank, Dana showed the dot to him. He recommended that she take her to an eye doctor. He called one and put Dana on the phone while he held Armani. They gave Dana directions on how to get to the eye doctor.

Dana left from that appointment, and in her car while driving, she would look back at Armani to make sure she was okay. Dana cried so hard while driving because it was just so much going on in her little girl's life, you couldn't imagine. Unless you read her eyes, and Dana believed she could, so she'll cried for her. She apologized to Armani a thousand times because for some reason, Dana believed she did something wrong to inflict her so much pain. She promised to keep her safe from any other harm and warm from the cold and prayed to God for guidance and strength.

The next morning, Dana took Armani to the eye doctor. The direction the receptionist gave her was perfect. She got there within no time. They took a small elevator; it only held four people at a time. Inside were Armani and Dana, an older woman, one man, and his wife. It was very packed. It was the second floor where everyone got off. They were all going to the same office. Actually, that was the only office open at seven thirty in the morning.

Dana was called right after handing in the forms she filled out. The pediatric eye doctor had black hair, was about five feet four inches, and was soft-spoken. He wrote down everything and put it on tape. He took all the names of the doctors Armani saw and promised to send each and every one of them information about the white spot in Armani's eye. He put drops in her eyes, then waited for an hour to get her eyes dilated so he could see it finally. When he did, he was amazed that Dana was able to see it. Well, he said it was a tiny spot of cataract. It was too small to block her vision, and she could see everything just fine. He said he will just watch it to make sure it doesn't get any bigger.

Armani was cooperative for a while, and then became aggravated with him opening and shining that light in her eye. He soon had enough information. He told Dana to make an appointment for two months. Then it will go to four months because he doesn't expect it to get any bigger or to be a problem.

Dana left there with one less problem on her mind. Driving home, she thought how she was going to tell Chase the news. He was going to take it kind of strange to hear his baby girl has cataract. When Dana got home, she called Chase on the phone and explained it as calmly as possible. He still didn't take it too well. He decided when he gets home this week, he's going to make sure he sees that white spot in her eye. Dana can hear he was still upset that he could not be home. He would continue to come home Sunday morning about 10:30 a.m. from Boston and go back to Boston on Tuesday night around 6:30 p.m. straight to work.

Dana would continue to work and take care of the children. She would run back and forth to the doctor's offices along with crying and worrying alone until Chase comes home. Most of the time before Chase gets home, Dana would already bounce back and wait for the next motion to happen. They spent a lot of time on the phone, where he helped her put things together until he got there.

It was just sometimes she couldn't wait to be held and told it's going to be okay.

Chase was great; he takes care of his wife and kids a hell a lot better than most men do who live in the same city. If she would have ended up with her ex, she would be divorced or widowed. He was self-centered, so selfish, he thought everything was all about himself. He had about eight kids all by different women. Thank god she didn't go down that road.

Chapter

FOUR

Gloria and Sam were Armani's godparents. They planned a post-baby baby shower on November 15. Armani was one month old. Dana was feeling better. Not too many of the family showed up. Her sister Cindy, Acee, Dana's mother, Gloria, Sam, Trudy, and Clare came late. Tina and her little friends (Sandra, Lisa, Kish, and Kim) came to the baby shower. Gloria had a big surprise. She had hired a male stripper. Dana was upset because she didn't want any man touching on her.

He asked Dana, "Who's the host?" Dana told him she was, but she just had a C-section, so don't even think about touching her in any way. Hopefully enough females would show up to enjoy the show.

Sam, being the only male forced to come because he was Armani's godfather, wasn't too happy about the show either. He sat in the Florida room and watched television. They waited for more women to show up, but of course, they didn't. So Gloria canceled the show. The stripper charged her for gas to get out there.

Dana was relieved. He was about six feet tall, around 200 lb., all muscle. He had fair skin, a nice clean bald head, biceps and triceps, and was all ready to pick up and flex and dance around. Those ladies missed out on a pretty good show with Mr. Fantasy. Dana was afraid of what he would have done to her basement. That would have been another highlight in her life.

Armani received gifts for a twelve-month-old. Everyone was afraid she would outgrow anything smaller. She was ten pounds already. Armani was held by Gloria, her godmother. Dana could not image her holding a holding a baby, but of course she knew how. She had three children of her own—eleven, sixteen, and an eighteen-year-old. Dana felt safe with her holding the baby. When she got the baby back, she smelled like perfume too strong for a baby. Dana ran upstairs to bathe her and change her clothes. That was a different sight to see of Gloria; Dana was used to seeing Gloria flirt her tail off. Having men anxious to get with her, they would almost do anything to get with her. One of Dana's friends, Mary, said Gloria should open a school to teach them all how to treat a man and take control of him. She was a lot of fun to be around.

Anyway, Dana was proud to have Sam and Gloria as Armani's godparents. As long as they had her back, Armani would be okay. That went for all her aunts and uncles and cousins. Everyone's heart was touched. How could someone so small have a problem so big? Crying hearts, it's called.

Thanksgiving was always Dana's favorite holiday. This year her sister Loren was cooking dinner at her house. Dana called Acee to tell her that they will not attend because she didn't want to bring Armani around the smoke. Acee yelled, "They can stop smoking for one day or go outside! Shoot. Or talk to Loren. I bet she will say the same thing."

Dana didn't want to inconvenience anyone at someone else's house, so she decided to stay home. But then Loren called and said, "Dana, bring my niece over. I will tell everyone they can't smoke, and if they can't understand that, to hell with them. That's my niece. We have to take care of her."

On Thanksgiving Day, Dana, Zeek, and Tina and her friend Donna came. They picked up Dana's mother Adele and her younger brother Roy from Brooklyn. Roy is thirty-five years old. He was very slow. Dana's mother treated him like a five-year-old. He went out and hung out late at night and drank beer and who knows what else. So he's no child in mind to Dana.

They arrived at Loren's house. Their sister Carol was there. She was a talker. As soon as they walked into the house, she said, "We cook this, we cook that." Then she yelled at Zeek, "Oh, you're not the baby anymore!"

Poor Zeek ran to the back crying. She had no idea what they went through getting him used to the new baby. Dana gave him a few hugs and kisses and cleared all that up. Armani stayed in her stroller. Dana kept Armani close to her.

There was no sign of smoke at all in the house. The house was absolutely smoke-free, and no one had a problem with it except one of Dana's brothers, Eddie. Eddie complained to the crew outside smoking. "Yeah, we have to come out here to smoke because of Dana's baby."

Acee yelled, "That's right, it don't hurt you to smoke out here for a day!"

He just sucked his teeth like a little girl.

They all continued to enjoy the day. Chase could not be there, so he spent the day in Boston with his sisters and their family before going to work.

Suddenly there was a knock at the door. Eddie looked through the peephole. He got all silly and excited. He shouted, "Oh shoot, it's security!" as he opened the door. Adele shouted, "Let Loren handle it! He ran out the door and closed it behind him. Acee went and got Loren. Eddie ran in. "I got this. I got to get my ID!" he yelled, knocking down Acee and Loren as they tried to go out to see what the man wanted.

He pulled Acee back and proceeded to show him his ID.

The man explained that he was sorry, he knew it's a holiday, but the man downstairs was complaining about the noise.

Loren him told him, "Thank you for the notice. Now, if you don't mind, me and my family are going to continue to enjoy our day."

And so they did even harder on the man downstairs head.

* * *

On December 19, Dana returned to work from maternity leave. Tina kept Armani and Zeek next door with the neighbor, especially on those nights when she would get prank phone calls whenever Dana left. Calls saying, "Hello, are you home alone? I'm going to kill you." It was a line from a scary movie. Dana didn't mind. She felt safe with the kids over there anyway.

After Wilma convinced Dana to get caller ID to find out which one of Tina's friends was calling, the calls stop. Wilma was very tall, about five feet eight inches, slim, fair skin. She always welcomed the kids to stay over to keep them safe, and Dana did the same for Wilma's kids. She had three girls. Keisha, sixteen years old, went to school with Tina; a four-year-old daughter who went to school with Zeek; and one who was nineteen and in college. That's when Dana started looking for someone to stay at home with the kids at night while she worked. The only person she could think of was Beatrice. So after the holiday, Dana would hire her.

In the meantime, Dana picked up Tina's cousins Jason and Karen around Christmas to keep her company. Besides that, Tina was working four days a week—Monday, Wednesday, Friday, and Saturday. Since November 18, she started complaining like a baby. "I have to work. I can't hang out anymore."

Dana just welcomed her to the real world and asked her how she thought Mommy felt. After working over ten years with no holiday or birthday off, it's not all fun. She reminded her that she just started.

On December 22, Beatrice started to keep the kids. She started off great, but then she started changing the way Dana did things. Like in the morning she would feed Zeek cold cereal before going out in the cold. Dana disagreed with this and argued with her to feed him a hot meal. She would bathe the kids at night before Dana woke up to go to work. One day when Dana went to pick Tina up from work, by the time she came back, she had already bathed the kids. When Dana looked at Armani's head, it was washed. Dana was amazed that she had washed out all of her cradle cap. When she asked how Beatrice did that, she held up a baby brush and smiled and said, "With this. I just brushed it out."

Dana said, "Wow!" Dana took Beatrice home that night and paid her. The next day, Dana noticed the scab had grown on Armani's head. Dana rubbed baby oil on it, and some of it came off, and Armani's head felt sticky. She realized that scab grew back in place of the cradle cap. Apparently, when Beatrice brushed the cradle cap out of Armani's head, it hurt her skin, and it scabbed up. Armani grew a bad smell on her head like pus. Armani would scratch it and pull her hair out.

Dana took her to Dr. Frank, and he told her to wash it with baby shampoo every day. He told her if it doesn't clear up to use a drop of Selsun Blue. The shampoo every day didn't work.

One evening, Tina and the kids stayed at Wilma's house. Tina came home the next morning when Dana got home from work and said, "Mom, Armani bust her head open and pulled out a bunch of her hair, and pus was coming out."

Dana picked Armani up and took her in the bathroom. Dana told Tina to hold her in both hands from her back so her head hung over the sink. Dana washed her hair with baby shampoo gently. Armani close her eyes in such a relief and enjoyed the wash. She licked her lips and let out a breath of relief. That wash felt good to her. Dana and Tina laughed at her. They had never seem a baby enjoy their head washed the way she did.

The next day, Dana and Chase washed Armani's hair. They used a drop of Selsun Blue. It took out the cradle cap and most of her hair at the top of her head. All Armani's pretty hair was gone. She looked like Danny DeVito. So Dana took her back to see Dr. Frank and told him, "I came to you for help, and now I have a Danny DeVito."

He explained sometimes that happened, but not to worry, it will grow back. Dana was a little upset, but all the nurses said the same thing. Armani had a really dry scalp, and her little head would flake up a lot. Dana tried everything for the dry scalp—baby oil, Vaseline. It cleared up, but slowly. Dana blamed Beatrice for the loss of Armani's hair. Chase convinced her otherwise. He felt she didn't mean to do it, that it was a mistake. Dana knew it was true. Besides, Armani had a real bad case of cradle cap. Her hair would have fallen out anyway.

Beatrice had just become a sanctified person. She put a lot of faith in God. To take care of Armani, she charged $50 a week, plus room and board and free food. All that was a good $150. Beatrice ate a lot. Beatrice, Tina, and Dana started a diet that they could never stick to. They would drink this diet tea to clean out all the food they had eaten for that day. They would eat a lot of food, then drink the tea like a laxative to clean it out. Dana knew without exercise, she was never going to lose the weight.

The holidays were coming up, and Pam was driving up with Chase. Dana was again undecided about going to Trudy's house to spend the holidays with the family. Dana's mom was complaining this time. She said that they can all stop smoking for the day. Dana didn't want to burden anyone, but she decided to go anyway. Dana baked cookies and put them in nice gift bags as gifts for everyone. Tina had to go to work, so Dana, Zeek, and Armani went to Trudy's house.

When she got there with her cookies, her sisters made her feel bad about her gifts. Dana went to the liquor store, and she brought her sister a bottle of wine and wrapped it. She also got her sisters Carol and Loren separate bottles of liquor and wrapped them as well. She brought her brother Clark and his girlfriend Anna ten lemons and cranberry juice and a ginger ale soda. They both were recovering alcoholics. Clark hadn't had a drink in three years.

Adele loved having the whole family together. All her daughters, sons, grandchildren, even her great-grandkids. Somehow and some way, she would have a gift for each and every one of her grandkids and great-grandkids. She didn't get her sons and daughters gifts because she had to get gifts for their children.

Chase and Pam were on their way up from Boston for Christmas Eve, and for sure they ran into a lot of traffic. Dana had to leave to go pick Tina up from work at 7:00 p.m. By the time Dana and Tina came back to the house, Chase and Pam were there. Pam was handing out cookies she made, and they all accepted them gracefully. Unlike the way they treated Dana when she handed them cookies. Chase was holding on to Armani like she was mistreated because Dana left her there with her aunts and uncles and grandmother to go pick up Tina from work.

Everyone started to exchange gifts early. No one liked to stay after midnight anymore. Once all the gifts were given out, they packed them up and left. Dana, Chase, Pam, and the kids stayed a little longer. Unfortunately, Dana had to leave from there to go straight to work. That was a hard thing to do, leave the family and go to work. Being a corrections officer was hard, working rotating days and steady midnights. The things you had to do to take care of your family. Chase worked as a corrections officer still, but in Boston, Massachusetts.

When Dana arrived at work, she parked her car in the parking lot after crossing the bridge. She walked through the control building to catch the bus to take her to her facility. She saw officers coming through with big trays of food. They were preparing for a Christmas party. No one from her facility had planned to do anything. She felt hurt that there was no type of unity or love for the holiday seasons. She was with a new line people with no one to hook up with for special events. Pretty soon that would all change. Dana thought she would not go to work again with no holiday spirit.

Finally her shift was over; it was time to go home to her family. When she got there, Tina had made a big breakfast along with hot chocolate and eggnog. She wanted everyone to eat first, then open up the gifts. Armani sat in her chair with her bright wide eyes looking at everyone. Pam videotaped everything. Tina got all the clothes she wanted. Zeek got all the toys he wanted; he was so excited, running from one toy to the other. He got racing cars, robots, and trucks. Tina bought him a talking teddy bear, and boy, did he get a kick out of that. She bought Armani this pink soft teddy bear.

Dana thought it was great for her; she sat it right in the chair next to her. Armani looked at it as Dana played with her. Armani laughed so loud; she enjoyed the attention. Chase got his silk pajamas he'd been crying for; he loved them. Tina bought her mother a pocketbook that she didn't even like, but she smiled and said thank you. Chase got her a jacket she wanted, but it was extra large. Dana knew she had gained weight, but now she knew he did too. There was nothing Dana opened that made her happy, only the smiles on her family's faces.

Well, Dana had to juggle between work and having someone safe to watch the kids during the week. Well, she worked it out until she and Chase went on vacation. They made absolutely no plans at all to go nowhere. They had no intention to leave or take Armani anywhere, so they planned to stay home. Chase started working on installing heat in the Florida room. Zeek came home from school with a bad earache. Dana called the doctor, and he said to bring him in. Armani had a fever, so Dana took her too.

After the doctor examined the kids, he said, "Zeek has an ear infection. I'm going to prescribe him something for it, and this one, Armani, I'm going to admit into the hospital. She might have a bronchi disease they have going around. She's congested."

Dana was in shock. She got herself together, packed up the kids, and went home. Chase had to stop the work he was doing.

Dana called the cardiologist and told him what was going on. Chase and Dana took Armani to the hospital where they did all kinds of test. They took fluid from her nose, x-rays, but couldn't find anything. This emergency doctor said if they let her go home, they had to bring her to see the pediatrician the next day, which they did and every day after that until the doctors felt it was safe.

Armani had this real nasty cough, and the doctors didn't want to give her any medication because it would speed up her heart rate. So Dr. Frank called the cardiologist, Dr. Boxx, and told him they needed to do something to help Armani's cough. Dr. Boxx decided to give her some cough syrup and some antibiotics to keep her from infections.

Chase and Dana took Armani back every other day, and her chest started to clear up. Finally they had a break from the doctors for a while.

Dr. Frank said to bring her back in a week. They wanted so much to take her to Boston to meet Chase's family. It was a hard decision, so they decided to go. Tina didn't want to go; she wanted to stay with Cindy. They let Zeek go with Tina to Cindy's house. This way if anything happened, they could do what they had to without worrying about him.

Dana packed up Zeek's bag and Armani and her bag. Tina packed her clothes. They put everything in the car. When it was time to leave, Tina, Dana, and Zeek were sitting in the car, waiting for Chase.

Dana said, "What is taking Chase so long?" She jumped out of the car and went stomping into the house. She looked in the bedroom. Chase was standing over the crib, holding Armani's sweater in his hand. Dana realized she forgot to get the baby. Chase was standing there confused, wondering why the baby was still in the crib.

Dana was so upset with herself. How could she forget to put her baby in the car? She made sure everything else was in the car. That's one she will never let go.

They dropped the kids off in Brooklyn and took the four-hour drive to Boston. By the time they got there, Armani had a fever and was coughing really hard. Pam had already prepared the room for them. They were going to leave to pick up something to eat, but the way she was coughing, they didn't feel safe leaving her, and Pam was too afraid to keep her.

Chase went out to get a thermometer because Dana left hers at home. When Dana checked Armani's temperature, it was 101°F. Chase wanted to take her to Boston Children's Hospital. Dana refused because she didn't want a whole set of doctors picking and poking at her baby. They would have to do everything over. Chase felt Boston had the best doctors. Dana thought maybe he's right, but she was very comfortable with the doctors she had. It was her gut feeling and wanted to take her baby home. Chase did not argue, and he started packing things up.

Pam yelled, "No, not now! It's twelve o'clock in the morning. By the time you get home, it will be four or five in the morning."

As long as Armani was sick, they didn't care. Dana gave Armani something for the fever. Pam made coffee for them, and they were back on the road.

Dana sat in the back with Armani to keep her comfortable and make sure she was okay. They talked all the way so Chase wouldn't get sleepy on the road. Once they got home, Dana took off Armani's clothes and put a cool cloth on her to break the fever some more. They all lay down and went to sleep.

In the morning, Dana called the doctor, and he said to bring her in. When they got there, Armani had no fever, and her chest was clear. They could not believe this. Dana thought maybe she broke the fever or something. They felt like fools, but also they thought it was better safe than sorry. Especially when it came to their baby girl.

Chapter

FIVE

Tina and Dana were in the basement getting ready to work out. Little Zeek was running around playing. Dana set Armani up in her chair right in front of them. Armani watched them when they swung their arms. She started swinging her arms and dancing with them; she'd kick the covers off her. That was really exercising to them. She was so cute, and all they could do was laugh.

When they danced toward her and got close, she burst out laughing and started kicking. Armani loved it; from the look in her eyes, they could see she really loved it. Tina would do it over and over again; she just got a kick out of it. They loved watching the expressions that she gave, especially her smile, from anything they did to her. When they put a camera in her face, she would give them a serious look. Like as if she was curious to what was that. She'd take the smile right off her face. Armani didn't like taking pictures.

One day Armani cried real loud. Dana ran over to check her. She had scratched her head. No matter how short Dana cut her nails, Armani would scratch herself. Dana would put socks on her hand. She wondered what made her cut her head and face so hard. Was it pain that she was feeling, trying to scratch it out? She didn't know what Armani was feeling. She would make really deep cuts. Dana put Vaseline on the cuts so they would heal really fast.

Dana still had a couple more days to spend home with the children. She wasn't sure if Beatrice was going to come back or not. Dana was supposed to have a day provider going on at the house. Dana and Gloria had got a group family day-care license together. Dana was too afraid to bring any other children around Armani, afraid she'll catch something. So she never started the day care. One lady begged Dana to keep her child. Dana felt so bad for her that she almost kept her child. She stuck to her guns because Armani was more important to her than anyone else. All three of her children were, but Armani needed more attention. Thank God Tina and Zeek were healthy.

Armani loved for them to sing to her; she would laugh so hard, and she'd start kicking her legs. One day Tina had her in the room with her watching a video. Armani started singing! Well, that's what it sounded like. She was singing real loud. Tina yelled, "Mommy, do you hear Armani?" Tina started laughing.

"Will you tell her to shut up?"

"She trying to sing! Can you hear her all the way in there?"

Chapter

SIX

On January 29, Dana took Armani to the cardiologist for her regular checkup. They did an EKG on her. When they finished, Dana stayed in the room till Dr. Boxx came in with his assistant. He said, "I want to do two things. One is admit her in the hospital, and two is get a chest x-ray on her 'cause I think she might have pneumonia. There is a lot of fluid in her lungs."

Dana's heart dropped. She looked at Armani, her wide eyes looking up at her. As if she was asking her, "What's wrong, Mommy?" Dana touched her little cheeks and rubbed them up and down and said to Armani, "If you only knew what was going on."

Dr. Boxx asked if she would like to call anyone. Dana replied yes, and he told her to use his phone since you couldn't bring your cell phone in the clinic. He picked up the receiver, pressed 7 first, and then the number.

Dana took out her cell phone to search for Chase's number. She could never remember the number since it was programmed in her phone. He picked up on the first ring, and Dana told him what was going on. He was debating on coming home right then, which he did. He would be home in four hours.

Dana went downstairs to the emergency room to see Dr. Rice for the x-ray. The x-ray was done, and they prepared Armani for admitting. They could not get a line in her, so they asked how Armani was eating. Being the doctor witnessing Armani suck down her bottle of milk, he felt she didn't need an IV. Dana was glad they didn't have to stick her baby with any needles. She would cry until Dana held her.

A couple with their son in the next bed from Armani waited outside the curtain while the nurse put the IV in him. She could feel her baby's pain as she held on to her husband with her eyes tightly close. As he screamed and cried, tears poured out between her closed eyelids. That is some feeling listening to your baby in pain.

The nurse told Dana to take Armani's stroller and put it in the car. While Dana was gone, the nurse took Armani's blood. When Dana returned, Armani was still crying. The doctor said, "Oh good, here's Mommy."

Dana picked her up, hugged her, and kissed her. She stopped crying. She looked at Dana again, her eyes saying, "Mommy, why did you leave me?" She was so glad her mommy was back.

When they went upstairs to her room, Dana carried Armani in her arms as she sat in the wheelchair. Chase got to the hospital just before they went upstairs. He said his daughter's health is more important, so he called out. Dana called out too for a personal emergency. When her supervisor asked her why, she told her the baby had a heart condition. She understood and said she will take care of it.

Armani was on the seventh floor in a room alone. The nurses were all very nice. One nurse asked what happened to Armani's hair. Dana told her she had cradle cap. She said, "Don't worry, that happens sometimes. It will grow back."

Dana was worried about her car being in the parking lot. The nurse told her to get her ticket validated before leaving to go home. They showed Dana how to turn the chair into a bed so she could stay all night.

By 8:00 p.m., Armani went to sleep. Chase and Dana left after telling the nurse they would be back in two hours. Dana needed something to eat. When she brought Armani to the clinic early that morning, she didn't eat breakfast, so she was starving. So was Armani. She drank her last bottle in the emergency room. They drove the cars back to the house. Dana showered and packed Armani's and her clothes. She packed the pink teddy bear that Tina bought her for Christmas and her pink blanket. Dana brought a hat to cover Armani's bald head. She packed baby oil to grease Armani's head, as well as T-shirts and pajamas. She put on comfortable clothes to sleep in and a toothbrush. She checked everything with Tina and Zeek to make sure everything was alright. She kissed and hugged Zeek and told him how much she and Armani loved him.

"Armani is not coming home tonight?" Zeek asked.

Dana told him, "Sorry, Zeek, she won't be home tonight. But she says to give you a kiss for her." Dana kissed his forehead.

He said, "Give her a kiss for me." He squeezed Dana's neck real hard and planted a big kiss on her cheek. "You heard that, Mommy?"

Dana said, "Yes, I heard that."

"You make the noise, okay, when you kiss her, Mum?"

She promised to make the noise.

At 10:00 p.m., Chase dropped Dana off and went back home.

Dana walked in the hospital and stop at security and told him her daughter was on the seventh floor. He told her to go right up. When she got to the room, Armani was awake. Dana felt really bad. Armani was screaming her head off. Dana wanted to yell at those nurses. She thought, *Are they crazy?*

Dana picked her up to console her, and she stopped crying. Dana was so glad that she could stay there with her to take care of her.

One nurse came in when she noticed Armani stopped crying and asked, "Are you Mommy?"

Dana said, "Yes, I'm Mommy."

Then the nurse left.

Armani was to start a medication today to see how she takes to it. The medication she was prescribed were named Heparin and Lasik. Heparin is a blood thinner to keep her heart from working so hard. Lasik was to drain out the excess fluid because they found out from the x-ray earlier that Armani had a leakage from one of her valves in her heart.

Armani had lost one pound, and they needed her to gain weight for surgery. When she had that cough, she wasn't eating much. So the plan was to get her big enough so they could replace that valve with a bigger valve that would grow with her. The smaller valve would not grow with her; it would have to be replaced in three months.

Dr. Silver had a nutritionist come and see Armani. She prescribed an infant-feeding module to add to her milk for extra calories. Her weight was taken every day, and they observed her reaction to the medication.

When Dana's cousin got the word Armani was in the hospital, she got on a Greyhound bus and came up that Friday. Dana was glad because staying at the hospital every night was exhausting; you couldn't rest. You had nurses coming in and out, taking Armani's vital signs or giving her medication. Whenever Dana heard Armani make a noise, she would jump up and pick her up. Dana pulled the chair out of the nurse's way so she wouldn't feel like she was on call.

Morning came, and Chase didn't get there until 10:00 a.m. Dana was hungry, tired, and stressed. Armani was calm; she seemed like she was fine. Every time Dana talked to her, she started smiling. You would not believe she was really ill with a congenital heart disease.

Finally Chase got there; Tina had made Dana a bagel with egg and cheese. Chase brought a pint of milk. Dana ate her breakfast, stayed for a while, then left Chase there with Armani. She went to the garage where he directed her he parked the car. She drove home, took a shower, and slept for a few hours. After she woke up, she went to the bus station to pick up Pam. They went to the hospital to relieve Chase. Pam wanted to stay at the hospital that night to give Dana a break. Dana was secure with the idea since Pam was someone she really trusted with Armani.

Chase and Dana left around 8:00 p.m. They went home and did some cleaning. Before Dana lay down, she called Pam to make sure she was okay. She said she was fine. She bathed Armani and changed her pajamas.

The next morning, Chase and Dana came back to the hospital. Dana made Pam some breakfast. They stayed until about twelve, then Chase and Pam left to go back to the house while Dana stayed with Armani. Pam helped Tina set up things for Zeek's surprise birthday party. It was his birthday on February 1. He was turning four years old.

Chase brought Zeek to the hospital to see Armani. Zeek was sitting on Dana's lap with Armani in her arms. Zeek said, "I want a new baby, a boy baby with hair."

Dana said, "Your baby sister's hair is going to grow back. She will be back with you soon, okay?"

"Armani, get well so you can come home," he said to her.

The nurse walked in and said, "Hello, you came to visit your little sister?"

"Yes," Zeek replied.

"How old are you?" she asked.

Dana told her to ask him when his birthday was.

"When is your birthday?" the nurse asked, waiting patiently for his response.

"February 1," he replied.

"That's today!" She looked confused.

Dana told her he had no clue that they were giving him a surprise birthday party. That they wanted to wait until she came on duty so they can spend about four hours with him for his party.

"Oh, okay! Well then, go ahead, she'll be okay. I will take good care of her," she said.

Dana said that once they put her to sleep, they will leave.

"Okay, give me a yell when you're leaving," Nurse Betty said.

"Okay, thank you," Dana said.

"No problem."

So Dana fed Armani and changed her, and then she fell asleep.

As Dana, Chase, and Zeek got close to the house, Dana called to tell Tina and Pam that they were on the way. The two of them set everything up while they were at the hospital.

When they got into the house, Dana told Zeek to go to the basement and get his toy. He opened the door and turned on the light switch. There was a group of kids, about ten of them, all neighborhood kids and his cousin Kerry.

She's the one who gave Dana the idea to give him a surprise party. She was all dolled up with her four ponytails. Cindy always dressed her so pretty. Red, white, and blue jeans outfit, her light skin, Indian complexion, and Chinese eyes. Dana used to tell Cindy her real daddy was Chinese.

Zeek was shocked to see all of his friends singing "Happy Birthday" to him. He acted upset, like he was spoiled, selfish, and he was crying a lot. Cindy and her husband brought Dana's mother. They wanted to go see Armani.

Right after they finished opening gifts, cutting the cake, and cleaning up, Dana drove Cindy, her mother, and Pam to the hospital while Chase and Ramon stayed at the house. When they got there, the nurse had already washed Armani up and put on her clean pajamas.

Cindy picked Armani up and held her. She said, "She looks like Armani. She doesn't look ill or anything. Look at her smiling at me. You glad to see your auntie? Dana, looked like you arch your eyes."

Dana replied, "No, girl, is you crazy? That's how they look."

Pam said, "Yes, they are so perfectly trim. That's how she was born. Her hair fell out from the cradle cap."

Dana said she tried to wash it as less as possible to keep her from catching colds. It turned out the cough she had came from the leakage from the valve. "Pam, I tell you, it looks like nothing is wrong with her. The doctor said the same thing," Dana said. She was laughing at them and smiling. "She is such a happy baby."

The nurse came in. "I hate to put you all out, but visiting hours is over."

Pam decided that she would stay the night, so Dana took her mother and Cindy back to the house.

Cindy and her husband and mother left Dana's house to go home. Dana wanted to go back to the hospital. So Chase took her back and waited downstairs for Pam. Pam was shocked to see her back. Dana told her to go back to the house so she can get some rest for her ride home in the morning. That was her excuse to stay with her baby. Pam said she came up so Dana can get some rest. Dana felt truly her best rest was with Armani. Dana would doze off here and there. When there was no nurse around her, she would sleep. That was all the rest she needed, but she had to be with her baby. Hold her little fingers, see her precious smile—that was her relief. Just to see and feel that she was okay, and after that, she will sleep a little.

Armani got a roommate, an eleven-year-old girl, and her mom stayed overnight in the room with her too. Chase felt uncomfortable about staying at night, so he would relieve Dana in the mornings. Dana would go home, shower, sleep, and spent some time with the kids. Especially after Tina told her that she missed her. When she came home, she tried to spend more time with them when they got home from school. Dana and Chase made it so that at least one of them stayed home at night with the kids.

That night, Armani's roommate left. So Chase stayed the night at the hospital with Armani. He said a nurse went on the empty bed and closed the curtain. He guessed she was resting on her lunch break. The next night, Dana told him she would stay. He said it would be safe for her to do the staying at night.

One day they got on Dana and Chase's nerves with all the same questions. They were tired of answering the same question. Chase yelled at them, "Why don't you just look in the chart?"

The doctor tried to explain that it was best to get their own information; this way there won't be any mistakes. Especially if the other doctors can't read each other's writing. It helps to prevent any errors, so they like to get their own information.

Armani was being released from the hospital on Tuesday. It was mandatory for them to go straight to a particular drugstore to get the medication that was prescribed for her. Dr. Skeet would not allow them to leave until he personally called and found a pharmacy that made up the prescription. Right away he took care of all of that.

Right before Dana and Chase left, he had the pharmacy call them in Armani's room for the prescription card number. By the time they got to the pharmacy, it was ready.

Chapter

SEVEN

Once Dana got home, she set up a program on how to distribute the medication and some new liquid stuff they gave her for extra calories. One of the nurses had trained Dana and Chase how to measure the medication in a syringe. They would have to train the babysitter when she came tomorrow. Dana trained Tina just in case she ever had to give it to her. She learned quickly. Dana explained that it was important to make sure they put a little extra calories supplement in her milk. It was important not to give her nothing more or nothing less.

Armani was happy to be home; she was smiling, happy to see her big brother and sister. Dana could tell they all missed each other. Chase decided to stay home with the family that night. They all tried to adjust to the new plans.

The next day, Dana went to pick up the babysitter, Beatrice. She was packed and ready to go. She got to the car. Dana helped her carry her bags and put them in the trunk.

Once they got into the car, she said, "Hello, first, if it is okay with the family, I would like to pray with the family."

Dana asked, "Armani too."

"Yes," Beatrice replied, "with the whole family together, if it's okay."

Dana said, "Sure, that would be good for all of us."

Dana began to explain Armani's condition.

Beatrice said, "The Lord is going to heal Armani, and she is going to be fine."

At that time, that wasn't the answer Dana was looking for, but if she had faith, she should too.

Dana knew deep down in her heart that every time she went back to those doctors, she prayed that Armani's condition would get better.

When they got to the house, first things first, Beatrice asked Chase if it was okay that she would like to pray with the whole family. He said sure; that would be good for them. "Where would you like to pray?"

She shook her head and said, "Anywhere."

Dana replied, "How about the living room?"

Beatrice agreed. "That will be good."

Dana called Tina downstairs. She always had an attitude when you called her out of her room. "What!" she whined.

"Beatrice is going to pray for the family. Come downstairs."

She went downstairs.

Zeek went in the living room. Chase had Armani in one arm, so Beatrice put her hand on his arm behind Armani's head. They all held hands. She began to pray. She went on asking God to put his hand on this family to watch over and protect, to touch Armani's heart. As she continued, her voice began to shake. She sounded as if she was crying and praying.

Dana felt a chill rush through her body. Beatrice's body started bouncing up and down, shouting, crying, and praying for a moment. They felt like they were in church. She started to calm down and ended with them all saying amen. Dana thought if it went on any longer, the anointing would have really started. She wanted to feel what Beatrice was feeling, just give herself to the Lord. Dana spent so much time praying to God herself late at night. Dana felt this was her sign from him. Beatrice was his guide to lead them in his direction.

They all went back to what they were doing. Dana thought they all had a big sigh of relief. A heavy burden was just lifted from her.

Dana took Beatrice to the kitchen to show her how to prepare the formula. Dana gave Beatrice the schedule on when to give Armani her medicine for the entire day. Chase and Dana had to go to work that night, so they needed to make sure everything was done right so their minds can be at ease while they were at work.

Dana would get off work in the morning, go home, and take a shower. Then she would give Armani her 9:00 a.m. medication and go to sleep. She would wake up at noon to give her more medication, and then again at 2:00 p.m. and then 6:00 p.m. Armani gets one dose of Lasik and a dose of Heparin. Dana would give her the 10:00 p.m. medication before she left to go to work. Beatrice would stay up till 12:00 a.m. for her scheduled medication and wake up at 6:00 a.m. to give that medication. If

Dana was off work, she would give her the 6:00 a.m. and 12:00 a.m. medications herself.

Feeding a baby that much medication constantly made Dana think, *Is it safe?* The doctors felt it will help her feel better. The fact that all of the medication she was taking could be damaging, affecting her liver and other organs in her body. All they could do was pray that wouldn't happen.

Dana was home one day discussing with Beatrice about giving Armani water. Dana kept a tight schedule on how Armani was feeding and getting her medication. When she checked the schedule, she noticed Beatrice had added water to the schedule. Dana asked her to please do not give her water. Beatrice insisted that everybody needed water to clean themselves out. Dana said, "Not this baby. She needs as much food as possible to gain weight."

Beatrice stated, "Well, as long as she's on my watch, she is at least going to get a little bit of water."

Dana got angry with arguing with her. She picked Armani up and went into her bedroom. She laid Armani on the bed and picked up a pillow. She sat it on her lap for a while, looking at Armani. She then picked it up over Armani and laid it on the side of her. She picked Armani up and laid her on the pillow. She started to sing one of her favorite songs called "Only for a While" by Anita Baker.

Dana thought about the terrible news that's on TV about the parents hurting and killing their own children. When she looked at her little angel, she thinks of the pain she is going through. What she wouldn't do to try to protect and shield her from pain.

There is nothing Dana can do but pray to God. She wished she knew someone who might even have a clue as to what pain Armani was going through. She's only a baby, a sweet, innocent little child. Dana prayed to God to please protect this child. Stop the pain, her pain, the family pain they all were suffering. Can this be a test that God is putting them through, to have them running and knocking on the church doors? Dana tried to think of a family that was going through worse to try to ease the pain she was going through. The thought of any baby or child going through any pain is unbearable to live with. Armani smiled when you talked or sang to her. She showed signs of a happy baby, except when you pointed a camera at her; the smile would then go away.

Dana started to go the church with Beatrice. She tried to open up her heart and accept the Lord. It seemed like every time she did, something went wrong. Dana felt she didn't give her soul; she didn't give her all. Dana gave more to Armani that she must have ignored its calling. Have you ever been whipped so bad you can't see straight? Well, that's what happened to Dana. She was so drained while taking care of Armani that church wasn't by any way the answer.

Dana took Armani with her and Beatrice to the hour of power. All the brothers and sisters along with the bishop got together and prayed for whoever needed to be prayed for. Dana went to the church on one Sunday service and asked to be saved, but it just wasn't in her heart. Not the way it should have been. Dana thought God knew she was using him to heal her baby. She prayed and prayed, but she felt God knew he would be used. That once he heals her baby, she would no longer call his name or go to church. God knew he had to prolong this healing, not make it easy to just walk away. She thought his plan was to make one stay in the light of Jesus forever.

Every time Dana took Armani to the doctor, things didn't look any better. She started to lose faith in God. What was his plan for her or for Armani? She desperately wanted some answers. Dana was losing her mind; she needed some help.

She went in another direction. She heard there was a place for people like her whose family was going through the same thing she was going through. Big Little Hearts for families who had a baby or child with a congenital heart disease.

Dana would go and speak to them to find out how to handle this, to make it easy for her or her family, to give them strength; they were all drained. She still had Beatrice keeping the word of God in her, giving Dana homework with scripture to read out of the Bible. Dana would read them every night while at work. She would pray every day, changing everything in her life.

Instead of babysitting, Beatrice was more inter-ested in Dana's family values. Dana always gave Zeek a hot breakfast before school. She wanted to give him cold cereal. Tina never traveled on the train alone to go to Manhattan. Beatrice wanted to let her go. She said she would take Tina and some of her friends to Manhattan, and they can find their way home. That's what she did to her son.

"And your son is fourteen years old. What did he accomplish from that? Is he a college expert in traveling or something?" Dana argued. "Listen, I don't want my child spending her time hanging out on no train in the city. She has plenty to do out here. Like keep her head in the books, go to the library. If she wants to shop, there's a mall out here. She can get her license. Or take a bus. But to just hang out in the city? I don't think so."

Beatrice gave Dana this look, "You're right," with her cat-shaped eyes that most men described as sexy. When someone speaks of her, they say, "Who? Beatrice with those sexy bedroom eyes?" She had fair skin, straight brown hair, and was thick boned. She had an annoying sharp speaking loud voice.

Beatrice responded, "You know, you're right because now he does stay out late on most nights."

Dana rolled her eyes to the top of her head and smiled. She said, "Now can we just let that idea go?"

Beatrice said, "Yes, we can."

Dana said, "Thank you."

Chapter

EIGHT

Thursday morning, Dana arrived home from work. She took a quick shower. Beatrice already had Armani dressed and ready for her cardiologist doctor's appointment. Dana invited Beatrice to join her. She felt Beatrice needed to know exactly what she was dealing with when it came to Armani.

While parking in a large lot for visitors and the out-patient clinic, Dana ran into an old supervisor who she used to work with. He was retired with a big stomach that hung over his pants. He smiled with his wild, crazy curly hair and thick black glasses. He said, "Yes, I'm retired."

Dana asked, "What you are doing here?"

He said, "I'm picking up a stiff baby. Yeah, I work for a mortician."

Dana frowned. "You picking up a dead body?"

"Yes," he replied. "Take my number."

Dana said, "For what? In case I ever have a stiff you can pick up?" She passed him a piece of paper and pen, and he wrote down his beeper number and headed on his way.

She took out the stroller as she always did. It was such a long walk from the parking lot and across the street. They walked about a mile before they reached the elevator to take it up to the fourth floor and a little walk from there.

Beatrice took Armani out the car. Dana set up the stroller and put Armani in it. They made sure she was warm and secure. They then headed to the long walk to the hospital clinic.

Dana was inside with Nurse Sandra while she examined Armani. She took her oxygen level and blood pressure. Armani was crying through the whole exam, especially the blood pressure as some of the nurses put it on too tight on her leg or arm. When Nurse Sandra tried to put it on, Armani was going wild. She didn't calm down until Dana held her in her arms.

Nurse Sandra said, "I don't think Armani likes me. I'm sorry, Armani, I don't mean to hurt you, okay, sweetie?" She asked Dana what kind of milk she drank.

Dana replied, "Isomil."

"Is it powder or ready to feed?"

"Ready to feed."

Nurse Sandra said, "Really? You should use powder, it's much cheaper." The nurse pulled out a case of milk and started packing it in Armani's bag. She said, "I see you got water in here."

Dana remembered seeing Beatrice put it in there. She didn't say anything because she wanted it to remind her to let the doctor talk to Beatrice about it. Dana said, "Oh yeah, the babysitter put it in there. Can you please explain to her about that?"

Nurse Sandra said, "Sure, where is she?"

Dana smiled. "She's sitting right outside."

Nurse Sandra asked what her name was. Dana gladly said, "Her name is Beatrice."

Nurse Sandra went out and came back in with Beatrice. "I understand you're giving the baby water?" Nurse Sandra explained that Armani didn't need it. "Milk has 50% water in it. This baby needs to grow, so she needs every ounce of food in her." She broke it down to her in a way that she would never give Armani water again.

Beatrice had a look of fear in her eyes. She kept a little turtle smile on her face the whole time. Only now she knew Dana meant business because she put the medical team on her. Who else would Beatrice listen to if not her?

When Beatrice left, Nurse Sandra said, "I probably scared the poor woman."

Dana replied, "No, she needed that."

Then the nurse looked at Armani's feeding schedule. "What happened this day? Looked like she had eaten ten in the morning and no more until 6:00 p.m.," Nurse Sandra said.

Dana said, "Well, her daddy kept her that day."

Nurse Sandra said, "Good, the next time bring him so I can read him too."

"I'm afraid you might not get to see him since we only come on Thursday."

"Well then, I'll leave him a note for you to post on the refrigerator. Then he can see it every time he feeds her."

Dana said, "That's a good idea."

Nurse Sandra also told Dr. Boxx about the water situation. When Beatrice and Denise were leaving, Dr. Boxx told Beatrice not to give Armani water.

Beatrice replied, "I know, no water. I promise. I learned my lesson." She then leaned in to whisper to Dana. "I think the nurse told the doctor on me."

On the ride home, Dana and Beatrice got into a discussion on their beliefs on what was going on about God. They both believed it was his way to bring Dana closer to God. Beatrice went on about how he brought her to him. She said back then the man whom she married, she didn't love him; it was all for money, being greedy. Things she did to get what she wanted. God took it all away and brought her down to nothing. That she had it all—the house, cars, money—and he worked it all down to nothing.

She ended up seeing a mental doctor. She was taking pills that really had her mind going. She started imagining things until she started going to church with her mother, and how she got saved. She didn't have any shoes or clothes. A sister from the church came up to her and said, "I got a pair of shoes that's too small for me. I think you can fit them." The shoes fit her perfectly, and she gave her some nice dresses. Things started looking up for her.

Dana decided that she, Chase, and the kids were going to visit her church together. She was hoping to let the bishop pray for Armani and the family.

Chapter

NINE

Chase came home on Sunday as he usually did and went straight to the basement bathroom. He took his shower before playing with the children. They all attended Sunday service in Brooklyn. Beatrice was surprised; Dana kept her promise.

The bishop asked, "Is there anyone out there who wants to be saved?"

Dana was shaking inside; she felt this was what she needed to do. She got up, walked over to Beatrice, and asked her to walk her up there. Beatrice took her hand; she started crying and hugged Dana with joy.

Dana stood there after all was done. Not one tear or feeling that the Lord had entered her soul. She feared she was doing something wrong. She felt scared and nervous. *Maybe that's the feeling*, she thought. She knew that she's in the right place that she has to keep coming until that feeling is there.

Dana went back to her seat and asked Chase, "Why didn't you join me?"

He said he didn't know she wanted him to come up with her.

She whispered, "Yes, it was something we should have done together."

Chase said, "This is a nice church, but it is too packed. It is too small for all these people."

Dana would like to join the church; it's not a bad church, but they are just visiting until they find a church home.

At the end of the service, the bishop prayed for who-ever came up for prayer. Dana and Chase took Armani up for prayer. Dana told the bishop that Armani had a con-genital heart disease. He said really fast, rebuking, "The devil is a liar. Dana smelled a strong scent of cologne as he reached to hold Armani. He was a young man, around early thirties.

He turned around and called for one of the sisters to come over. He started to pray. He asked the Lord to touch Armani and bless everyone and everything and all the doctors. "Bless the medicine, her parents, all that has part to help with her healing."

Dana felt a big stomp in her heart. She had a very strong and good feeling. Something has happened; she wasn't sure what, but she felt it.

When they got home, Dana cooked her favorite dish, shrimp scampi with vegetable lasagna and biscuit. She made baked chicken. An old friend of Dana, Linda, came by the house with her new boyfriend. It was her first time ever meeting Chase and the kids. They talked about old times.

Linda enjoyed Armani and Zeek, and so did her friend. Linda wanted to have another baby in which she convinced her friend to agree to have one. Dana and Linda used to sing together. Linda wanted to get back into singing. But Dana did not want to. She wanted to get into a church and join a choir or maybe start her owns.

Linda always had her mind set on becoming a big star. Dana lost that dream; her children were her future. If they have that desired, she will support them all the way. Dana told her she will only go back to singing in a church. Linda left with the thought to go into Gospel singing. She said she will think about because her boyfriend was trying to get her into church anyway.

Chase was up early in the morning going through some papers. Calling the investigator, he found out he was held over from the job. Stress he never wanted Dana to see him in. He got dressed and went into the garage to clean it.

Dana knew he was upset; she knew he was at his breaking point. He was about to lose it knowing his daughter was sick and he couldn't be home. To help take care of her and relieve some of the pressure was killing him. He talked about taking any job, even a drop in pay. Dana refused to allow him to do that; she knew it would just add on to the situation. They had the house, bills, food, and children to take care of. Every step they make must be the right step. They had to hold on to faith and continue the struggle.

Chase blamed himself. Dana wondered what she did wrong. Chase questioned Dana since Zeek and Armani were three years apart; he wondered if Dana used some type of birth control pills in between that he had no knowledge. Maybe her diet had something to do with Armani's condition. It came to the point where Dana began to question herself. Dana heard a rumor that her older sister blamed Dana for eating the wrong foods. Maybe she did, working on that cold post every night. She thought about the medication she was taking in the beginning. Maybe the drinking water, or maybe her strange craving likes the taste of crewing toilet paper. Was it the stress of hoping and praying for her husband to be home for good? She thought about everything, even picking up Zeek when he fell and hurt himself. Was it genetic? Dana thought if she did do anything wrong, only the Lord knew.

Chapter

TEN

Beatrice called the house one night after Dana went to work and spoke to Chase. She said, "Chase, I think you should know, your wife doesn't get any sleep. She comes home from work in the morning, takes a shower. Comes in the room and takes the baby from me. She breaks her sleep by setting her alarm clock. Dana is up at 10:00 a.m., 12:00 p.m., and at 2:00 p.m. to give Armani her medication. When she's driving in the car, she spent most of her time looking in her mirror back at Armani instead of the road. You know, Gloria paid for you two to go on a weekend trip to the Poconos. I'm willing to keep the kids. I think you should convince her to go, just you and her alone. So she can get at least one good night of sleep."

Chase told her that he didn't know if Dana will leave the baby.

Beatrice blurted out, "Chase, your wife doesn't get any rest, and if she continues, she's not going to be well enough to take care of Armani. I think she needs more help than Armani do right now. Listen, think about it. Me and Gloria already talked about it, so between me and Gloria, the kids will be taken care of, okay? Let me know. Goodbye."

When Dana got home from work that morning, she took her shower, then she took Armani from Chase. Chase watched her, then he said, "Honey, why you don't get any rest when you get home from work during the day?"

Dana snapped back and yelled, "What!"

"Why you don't get any rest if Beatrice is here with the baby?"

"Because I want to take care of my own baby," Dana said.

"Beatrice called last night and told me you be driving while looking back at Armani in the mirror."

Dana laughed and said, "She's right, I do. I just want to make sure Armani's okay. I can't knock that."

Chase then asked, "So are we going on this trip Gloria planned for us?"

Dana, surprised, said, "What, you honesty thinking about going?"

He replied, "Why not?"

"What, we going to take Armani with us, right?" she asked.

Chase said, "If you want to. It's up to you. We have time to think about it."

The phone rang. Dana picked up, and it was Gloria.

"Hello, Dana what did you guys decide to do? Are you going on the trip?"

"If we go, we're going to take Armani with us," Dana told her.

Gloria yelled, "No! You two go by yourself. You need the time away. The trip is already paid for you two. Go ahead and enjoy yourself."

Dana asked her, "Are you going to look after Armani?"

Gloria said she couldn't on Friday, but she would keep her Saturday and Sunday. "Come on, Dana, you go ahead and give you and Chase a break."

"I will think about it and let you know."

Dana talked to Beatrice that if they decided to go on the trip, would she promise to keep the kids in the house? Beatrice argued, "Stop locking this child in the house! Let her out and gets some air. The kids will be fine, I promise." She would keep them on Friday. Tina would go to her aunt Cindy's house to hang out, and Armani and Zeek would hang out at Dana's mother's house. They would pick Tina up later.

"Don't call us 'cause I'm not going to pick up the phone. I don't want you worrying every day. Just go and relax and get some rest."

Still after talking to Beatrice and Gloria, Dana still needed to feel secure about leaving her baby. She called Cindy, her sister. Dana said, "Cindy, I wish you were able to take care of my baby. Will you call me when you drop Tina off?"

Cindy told her not to worry; she would be with Gloria on Saturday and that she was pretty sure she knew what to do if anything went wrong. Janise, Cindy's friend, yelled to the phone, "That's nice, Dana! You have some good friends looking out for you. I would take advantage of it. You should go. I mean, when was the last time you laid down and got you a good rest?"

Dana could not remember.

Janise said, "Then go! It will be good for both of you."

Mayra told Dana, "You should go. It will only be for two nights. If you go and don't feel good about the first night, then go home."

Dana asked her if she would she check on the kids for her. Mayra promise she would and convince her it will be alright.

Then at work, Dana talked to a coworker named Barnes. Barnes said, "Girl, I could not begin to imagine what you are going through. This must be tough on you, but I know one thing. You need some rest. You come in here drinking that coffee to stay up all night, and then go home to deal with the baby. If she's taking medication that many times a day, you can't be getting any type of rest. I do think you should go, as long as you got responsible adults caring for her. You know Gloria is going to make sure her goddaughter is taken care of. That is for sure. I know Gloria. So, girl, go and get some rest."

Dana's meal relief came to relieve her for meal named Samantha. She asked Dana, "Hey, girl, how's it going and how's the kids?"

Dana began to tell her about Armani's condition. Samantha began to cry. She thought Dana's situation was so sad. That a little baby was going through so much. She understood why Dana didn't want to leave her baby. She said she wouldn't want to leave her baby either. But she told Dana that she would need her strength so that she could care for Armani.

Dana finally decided that she and Chase would go on the trip without Armani. She told Beatrice that she decided to go, but if anything went wrong to call Gloria. "Keep Armani one night, and Gloria will come and get her the next night. Then you can keep Zeek. Tina can stay home. Sunday Zeek will go to church with you. I will call—"

Before Dana could finish her sentence, Beatrice yelled, "No phone calls, okay!"

Dana told Tina, "You make sure you answer the phone."

"Don't worry, Mommy, I will answer your calls," Tina said.

"Thank you," Dana replied. She picked up Armani and said, "You know, Armani sounds congested."

Beatrice yelled, "Oh no, there you go again, trying to get out of going on your trip!"

"But she is, don't you hear? Listen!"

Beatrice put her ear to Armani's chest and said, "I don't hear anything. Look at her, she's laughing at you. Yes, your mommy trying to use you to stay home. If she was congested, you could hear it. She probably needs to go out for some fresh air. You keep her locked up in this house."

Dana said, "Yeah, you're right."

Beatrice asked, "Where are you going?"

As Dana dressed Armani, she said, "To visit a friend."

Beatrice smiled. "Good."

Dana smiled back and said, "Besides, her husband is a nurse."

Beatrice rolled her eyes and said, "Oh lord." She laughed. "Go ahead, take her to more doctors."

"He a nurse," Dana said as she put on her coat, then wrapped up Armani and walked out the door. She took a nice slow drive to Myra's house. When she got there, she took Armani out of the car, walked up to the door, and rang the doorbell.

Jack opened the door and yelled, "Hello, Mrs. Frazier! Myra, Mrs. Frazier and the little one is here. Oh, how cute!" He took Armani out of Dana's arms, walked her over to the couch, and started taking off her coat.

Myra picked her up. Armani looked at her with a serious look like "Who are you." So Jack took her from Myra, and Armani started smiling.

Dana said, "Oh, Myra, he's getting the baby fever."

Jack said, "Well, why not. Hey, look at you, little cutie, oh, look at these big hands."

Dana said, "She sounds congested to me. Can you check?"

He listened to her chest and said, "She sounds find."

"Are you sure?"

Jack gave her a little smile. "Trust me, if she was, I would have heard it."

Dana said, "Okay, I just wanted to make sure."

He passed Armani back to Myra. Edwin came in. He walked over and looked at Armani. Armani began to smile. Edwin blushed, then Armani looked at Myra and smiled.

Myra said, "Oh, there she goes, smiling at me," and Myra giggled. "I finally deserve a smile after seeing the two men first."

They all laughed.

"I'm cool now," Myra said.

They sat and talked for a while. Suddenly, Dana realized that it was a quarter to six, and it was almost time for Armani to take her medication. When she noticed she didn't bring it with her, she quickly began to dress Armani to take her home.

Jack carried Armani to the car. He was such a gentleman. Myra and Dana are both pleased with their choice of husbands.

Dana got Armani home just in time to give her medication, feed her a bottle, and take a nap. Dana picked up the phone to tell Gloria that she would take the weekend trip. Gloria was glad she decided to go.

Chapter

ELEVEN

It was late at night. Dana couldn't sleep; she was too busy thinking about what could have gone wrong with Armani. At three o'clock in the morning, she thought of Pam. She was off in the morning, and she wouldn't mind if she called her.

She picked up the phone and called her. "Hello, Pam?"

"Dana? Yes. What's wrong?"

Dana asked her, "Do you remember the dreams I told you about when I was pregnant with Zeek?" Dana had a double dream—a dream within a dream. She was asleep, and Zeek named himself. She woke up, and Chase was lying next to her. She woke him up and told him that the baby named himself. He asked her what was the name, and when she told him, he said, "That's a biblical name." Then she woke up from that dream. Chase was there lying next to her. She woke him up, and this time, as she told him about the double dream, she could not remember the name, so they named him from the Bible—Isaac. Zeek became his nickname.

When she was pregnant with Armani, she dreamed twice that she already had the baby. In one of her dreams, she didn't know where the baby was, but was looking at her flat stomach, looking for the baby. The second dream, God was talking to an angel, telling her to look over the baby.

Dana asked Pam, "Do you think that was a message telling me that the baby was going to be ill? Was it a premonition or a vision of the future?"

Pam said, "I remember when you first had those dreams, you would call me or Cindy late at night to tell us about it. Is that what got you up at three in the morning now?"

Dana told her, "Yes, I wanted to make sure you remember them."

Sometimes she would call Myra since she worked midnights. She was sorry for calling her that night. Pam told her she remembered the time very well. She said, "Hey, why you don't try thinking about these things a little later in the morning, like eleven o'clock or so?"

They both laughed.

Dana got the message and told Pam to go to sleep, that she will talk to her in the morning. She hung up.

Dana laid her head on the pillow right next to Armani and stared at her chubby little face. She slept so peacefully; her head moved, and she didn't even wake up. Her little lips smacked together like she was sucking on a bottle. It tickled Dana to see that. Dana put her finger in Armani's hand. She closed her hand, holding on to Dana's finger as she slept.

Dana easily fell into a deep sleep, maybe not for long, but just long enough to gain a little strength to make it another day.

Armani was doing well with the medication and food. Dana spent a lot of time arguing with Chase and the babysitter about making sure Armani ate and with the babysitter Beatrice telling her how to run her family. Poor Tina, she didn't really have a life. Everything changed since Armani's been sick.

Dana joined the big heart little heart group. She attended one meeting, which they met the first of every month. Everyone introduced themselves. They explained what their child was going through. Every one of their children already had surgery. One lady's child had surgery and was getting ready for another one. One couple kept putting off their child's surgery. Bobby, the guy who ran the program, his son had surgery when he was a baby and was now six years old. The woman Dana spoke to who told her about the program, her daughter was fourteen years old. She didn't make it to the meeting that night.

Bob and Dana both dealt with the same Dr. Steven that Dana switched from. Dana told them about how that doctor spoke to her and Chase. Tom said it was funny that Dana said that because six years ago, if he had not listened to her, his son would not be alive today. That he had reported her to the head of the hospital cardiologist. Bob gave Dana a book and a pamphlet to help her understand about congenital heart disease.

Tina and Dana both went to one of the meetings. One of the mothers asked Tina how she felt. It turned out Tina and the lady's sixteen-year-old daughter felt the same way. She gave Tina her phone number and told her to call and talk to her daughter if she felt like it. They both felt like they had no life because their mothers didn't go anywhere or did anything but spent most of their time with the babies. This was true. Dealing with Armani was exhausting.

Chapter

TWELVE

D ana and Chase were packing and preparing for
their weekend trip. The one that Dana really
wanted to cancel, but forced herself not to give
Beatrice a chance to say, "I told you so." Beatrice knew
that Dana was looking for an excuse not to go. Dana
planned to call her bluff.

Friday was here, and they were packed and ready to
go. Chase left his car for Beatrice to get around in. They
took a two-hour drive to the resort, checked in, and went
up to the room. Dana pulled out her cell phone and called
home. There was no answer. She hung up and called
Cindy. Cindy picked up and told her that they came by
and dropped off Tina, and Beatrice said she will be back
later to pick her up.

Dana complained, "Beatrice told me not to call. Is
she crazy?"

Cindy told Dana to stop worrying, that she will
make sure her nieces and nephew are okay.

Dana hung up.

Chase told Dana, "We just got here. It's only been two hours. Put the phone away and try to enjoy the trip."

She cried. "It's not easy."

"I know it's a hard thing to do, but I want to see you relax, just a little."

So she lay down to take a nap to rush the day away. She woke up a couple hours later and took a shower. They went out to dinner. After they finished eating dinner, Dana asked Chase if they can pick up something to drink. They drove around to search for a liquor store. They brought three different bottles of liquor.

When they got back to the room, there was a gift from Glenda—a bottle of wine and two crystal glasses with bubble bath. Dana got as drunk as she could to relax and enjoy the evening. While being a little drunk, she still had to pick up the phone. Chase gave in and told her to go ahead and call. She needed to make sure everything was alright.

Dana called Cindy. Cindy confirmed that Beatrice picked up Tina and that she and the kids were on their way back to the house. Cindy told her, "So now you can relax."

So she did. They had a good night secret untold.

The next morning, they woke up and took a shower. They went out for breakfast. After breakfast, they went back to the room. They got back in the bed and took a nap. They then woke up, went out to the mall, found a movie theater, and took in a movie.

Dana called Gloria, and she said she had Armani and that her medication was still on schedule. Dana was much more relaxed because Gloria didn't mind if she called to check on the baby. Gloria filled Dana in on everything.

Dana enjoyed herself the rest of the day. They did a little shopping and bought a treadmill. Early the next, they showered and packed everything in the van and headed home. Dana was so grateful that the weekend was over, only to get back home to her children.

When they got there, Beatrice was cleaning up the house. They took Beatrice home first. As soon as they arrived to Gloria's house to pick up Armani, Dana grabbed her, hugging and kissing on her, crying that she missed her so, so much. Gloria packed up Armani's bag.

They went home. Dana was so glad to be home with her children. She missed them all. Especially Armani after Gloria told her that Armani had a reaction when she gave her the medicine. Dana kept hearing congestion from Armani, and this time it didn't clear up. So she decided in the morning she was going to call the doctor. Chase didn't think anything was wrong, but Dana didn't feel right about it. Chase never liked those doctors sticking and poking at her anyway. So to him, as long as Armani looked good and was smiling, he was happy.

Armani started drinking her whole bottle of milk. So Chase was pleased. He said, "Look how good she's eating." He never saw her eat so much since she got sick the first time. Dana told him that when Armani eats a lot, she's overworking her heart. It's like heavy foods like cholesterol that clogs up her artery. To Dana, every time Armani's appetite got big, something goes wrong. Yes, she was eating a lot. Chase was happy. Dana was too, but she was worried because she could still hear the sound of congestion in Armani's chest. Dana wasn't too happy, so she kept a very close eye on Armani all night.

The congestion still didn't clear up, so she called Dr. Boxx and told him she was worried about her congestion. Dr. Boxx asked Dana how she felt about bringing her in for an x-ray. Dana said fine and that she would feel better knowing what's going on. Chase complained he didn't like her taking all those x-rays. He said he heard on the news about it causing some type of illness.

They took her anyway. The x-ray showed her chest was clear. They gave her all kinds of tests, then assumed she had an upper respiratory infection. She was admitted into the hospital. Dr. Boxx told Renee, one of his patient's mothers who now worked with him. Renee was the one who invited Dana to come to the Big Little Hearts meetings. She came to the room and met Dana. They became good friends.

Dr. Boxx increased Armani's medication and planned to do a catheterization. He felt now it's time to do something to help her. The whole team of pediatric cardiologists had a meeting to discuss her condition and a plan to help her. The catheterization was schedule for March 17. Armani went home two days later, March 12, a Thursday. The babysitter came over a little after Dana left for work. Dana worked the post 13 control. The officer who worked the 13 dorm was on leave for her birthday. To top it off, it was the morning of Friday the thirteenth.

It was kind of scary to Dana; it was too many 13s. On the 13 side, one inmate had a seizure. When it stopped, he got up and almost fell, and the other inmates caught him. The count was messed up twice. A fight broke out at three in the morning. Dana's gloves were stolen from her locker. Dana was more than happy to hurry up and get out of there.

On her way home, she stopped by the store to pick up some Pampers, milk, and food. When she got home, the babysitter was dressed and ready to go. Dana took her shower, then the babysitter left. Dana took Armani and put her in the bed with her. Dana played and sang to her. Armani was laughing; she even tried to sing with her. Dana was having such fun with her.

Dana began to feel tired. It was 11:45 p.m., and she waited till 12:00 a.m. to give Armani her medication before she fell asleep. She washed her hands, got the medicine, and gave it to her like she always did. Once Armani took it, she started coughing like she had trouble breathing. The phone rang. Dana picked up. It was Gloria. Dana told her what Armani was doing. Gloria had kept Armani twice while Dana was at work, and she said she did something like that to her when she kept her. "Take her to the hospital."

Dana begged Gloria to come with her because she was so tired. Dana had stayed at the hospital the two nights on Wednesday and Thursday, then went back to work Thursday night. So she didn't get any rest. Gloria said she would meet Dana there.

Dana called the hospital, and they said to bring her in. Dana quickly got dressed and dressed Armani. She put her in the van and drove off, not thinking straight. She got one block and looked back in the mirror at Armani. Her mouth was open, and her eyes rolled back to the top of her head. Dana started yelling. "Armani, stay with me!" She knew she couldn't stop to call an ambulance now.

Dana started running lights on the twenty-miles-per-hour streets. She was doing at least 60 to 70 mph, hoping a police would pull her over. Dana continued to run light after light, praying to get a police escort. But it never happened.

She made it to the hospital. She ran to the triage nurse and yelled, "The baby is having trouble breathing!"

She sat Dana down and asked her some question. Then they took Armani into the back. Dana started undressing Armani to help the nurse. The doctor held her down to find a vein. Dana yelled to them to get Dr. Boxx from pediatric cardiology as she had a heart condition. Someone made the call. Dana heard someone yell, "This child needs to be worked on immediately!" They couldn't find a vein. Dana told them she just left the hospital yesterday, and they had trouble getting blood then.

One doctor came down and said he was familiar with her condition and broke it down to them. He pulled Dana out of the room and explained that they needed to get a line open from a main artery in her leg. He told Dana that she couldn't be present for the procedure and asked her to have a seat outside.

The triage nurse escorted Dana to the triage area where she sat there with the nurses. The nurse offered Dana a cup of coffee. As she drank it, she told them what happened on her ride there. How she was running streetlights, praying for a police to pull her over so she can get escorted.

While waiting for the doctor to finish the procedure, two patients came in. One was an older lady having an anxiety attack. The other patient was a little girl who had cut her hand in the playground. Dana said to the nurse sitting with her boy, "I wish that's all Armani was here for."

The other nurse replied, "Yeah, but a lot of people don't see that."

The nurse sitting with Dana went back to see if they had finished. Then she took Dana back. When Dana looked at Armani, there were so many things they had put on her. Dr. Boxx was there working on her. As Dana was looking in on them, Dr. Boxx stopped and said, "Mrs. Frazier we have some more sticking to do. Wait outside."

The nurse sat Dana in a chair right in the room next to her. The curtain was closed. There were so many around her working. Dana listened as she heard them yell give me this, give me that. Then she heard them pushing something down her throat. She heard a choking sound. Dana began to cry continually. Someone passed her a box of tissues.

Dr. Boxx yelled, "We have to get her upstairs! Is the room ready yet?" Someone yelled yes.

"The elevator's waiting, where's the mother?"

"She's right here. Let's go, Mrs. Frazier."

They wheeled Armani to the elevator on the bed. They all rushed to the elevator. The bed was surrounded, as it was when they first got there.

The group of doctors and nurses and Dana went up to the Pediatrician Intensive Care Unit. Dana was sent to the waiting area, and a social worker came in to talk to her. She tried to be as much help as she could. Dana could not remember one phone number. She called her mother four times before she could get it right. Dana asked her mother to call Chase and tell him what was going on. Dana and the social worker were trying to talk when a man got on the phone and was talking so loud, they could not hear each other. Dana began to yell at him. The social worker suggested that they go to the office.

When they went in, Dr. Boxx said, "Here, you ladies can use my office."

While Dana and the social worker were talking, Ruth came in. Dana was so glad to see her. She ran to give her a hug. Ruth asked Dana if she called her job. Dana told her no. Ruth suggested that she do it now because she would not be thinking about it later.

Dana called her job. Officer Regina picked up. Dana told her that she needed a personal leave for the night because she was in ICU with her daughter. Officer Regina repeated the message to the captain. The captain asked her, "Well, is she going to be in ICU all night because I do not have enough officers to cover the post tonight. Tell her to call back before 10:00 p.m." The officer put the phone on speaker because she didn't want to relay his message.

Dana heard him and asked Officer Regina, "Why is he saying that? Tell him I'm not in Pathmark. I'm in ICU, for God's sakes, and by ten tonight, I'm not going to be thinking about that place!" Dana got upset and started crying and yelling. "What is wrong with him?"

The captain told the officer to tell Dana to take eight hours comp and not to worry, to go ahead and get herself together.

They hung up.

Ruth started shaking her head and told Dana maybe he don't know what ICU is. They went back to the waiting room. Gloria finally made it there. Dana told her what the captain had said when she was trying to get the time off. Gloria ran to the phone and called him and cursed him out. He tried to explain to her, that he gave her the time off, but Gloria didn't care. She reported him to the warden and got him in trouble. Dana was glad Gloria fought that fight for her because she was too weak to fight it herself.

Finally Armani was stable, and they were able to go in and see her. She was on a respirator hooked up to an EKG, and all kinds of tubes were hooked on her. She was in this small room alone.

Her nurse Renee told Dana to go home and get some rest. Dana refused. The nurse told Dana that she won't be able to sleep in the room, but she can sleep in waiting room, but she wouldn't get much rest in there. She told Dana, "You need your rest to take care of the baby, and I will call you if there is any change."

Gloria insisted that she was going to go home. So Dana looked at Armani and gave in and said, "Alright, I'll go home."

Dana went home and started cleaning. She did anything to keep her mind busy. BJ, Gloria's son, started cooking a simple meal. Gloria brought some beer for Dana to drink to help her sleep. BJ said, "I finished cooking, now you can go to sleep."

Dana said, "Okay, I will make me a plate, drink this nasty beer, and go to sleep." That is exactly what Dana did and fell to sleep at 10:30 p.m. while Gloria and BJ stayed in the room.

The phone rang. Tina picked up and took the phone to Dana. "Mommy, this is the hospital."

Dana jumped up and grabbed the phone. Dana's voice was shaking. "Hello!"

The nurse said, "Mrs. Frazier, we would like for you to come in. Armani took a turn for the worse."

Dana's heart dropped to the bottom of her feet.

"Do you have someone to bring you in?"

Dana remembered Gloria was still there. She told her yes. Gloria drove her to the hospital. Dana decided to call Chase. The whole hospital was talking about how he made it there in two and a half hours on a four-hour drive.

When Dr. Boxx came out, his hair was straight on top of his head. Dana asked him what happened; it looked like he was in a fight. He responded, "Your daughter won't let me get any rest." He told them that Armani was stable. It was four in the morning, so he told them to go home and get some rest.

They all left. Gloria and BJ went home since Dana had Chase.

Chapter

THIRTEEN

Dana tried to rest until ten in the morning. Then she got up and started getting herself together. Chase thought that everyone should go to the hospital. Chase, Tina, Zeek, and Dana went to the hospital. When they got there, Zeek was not able to go into the room. Chase stayed in the waiting room with him. Dana didn't think Chase was able to handle seeing his daughter like that. He wouldn't stay in the room long.

Tina went in the room with Dana. She tried to be strong. Dana didn't know till later that Tina couldn't handle seeing Armani with all those tubes in her sister either. So they took the kids home. Dee and Rob called and said they wanted to go see the baby and for Dana to meet them there. Rod was Dana's brother and Dee his wife. They arrived at 6:00 p.m. Dana was already in the room. Dee and Rob walked in. Dee looked at Armani as she walked in with a scary look on her face; she tried to be strong.

Armani was naked with a catheter tube to catch her urine. She had a tube with a pacemaker in case it was needed, so they wouldn't have to use the electric shock anymore. On her other thigh was another line that had the medication. There was strong heart medication, Lasik, sedation to keep her from feeling the pain from the respirator. So many medications you would want to cry. It was about eight tubes of medication being pumped into this little baby.

At 7:00 p.m., the nurse shift was changing, and Nurse Sally was getting ready to leave. She told her relief that she took the covers off Armani because her temperature was a little high. When Dana held her hand, it was cold. When Dee saw the nurse carefully touching and changing Armani's medication bag, she took her other hand. The nurse carefully put tape and the names of each medication on the lines. Rob told her that was a great idea; this way the lines wouldn't get mixed up.

Gloria came in the room. It's only supposed to be two people in the room at a time, but Nurse Jane said she didn't mind. It was up to the nurse. Jane was a very nice Italian lady with long brown hair and was a very fast talker. She said she was going to let Armani come out of sedation for a while.

Dana was glad to hear that. She wanted to see her baby awake so badly. As she held her hand and spoke to her, Dana would see her jump and kick open and close her eyes. Dana bent over to sing one of Armani's favorite songs to her, "Only for a While." Her eyes would open up real wide. Her body shakes got stronger.

Everyone noticed Armani's response to Dana's singing. Dana's heart jumped; she felt afraid. As she continued to sing to Armani, tears flowed down Dana's eyes. It felt so good seeing her respond after her lying there, not moving all day. With Armani being alert, her heart rate started to go up. To bring it down, the nurse had to sedate her again. Dana just wanted to take all those tubes and the respirator out of her mouth and be able to pick her baby up and hold her tight.

Armani began to relax. They all felt a little saddened from this unresponsive movement. Visiting hours was over, and it was time to leave. Well, not the mother. Dana could stay all night if she wanted to. Gloria and Dee and Rob left. They had a dinner to go to and had to get directions from Dana on how to get there.

Dana returned back to the room when Armani started having irregular heartbeat. Jane called in the doctor. Dana panicked. There were six nurses, doctors, and aides in the room. They wanted Dana to stay; not one time did anyone ask her to leave. Dana wouldn't dare leave now. Dana started to fall asleep. They did ask her to go lie down in the visitor's room where there was an open-up chair. They promised to come and get her if anything happened. They didn't want her to sleep in the room because it was small, and if anything happened, they would have to keep moving her out of the way.

So she did, but she was in and out all night because Armani had irregular heartbeats all night. At 7:00 a.m., Sally came to relieve Jane. Sally convinced Dana to go home and get some rest. She said Armani was going to have these irregular heartbeats. Dana needed to get her rest so she will have strength to continue to care for her when all this is over.

Dana agreed, so she went to kiss Armani and left. Dana knew she could call anytime of the day to check on her. Dana went home and took a shower. She wondered why no one looked for her, but Chase assured her that they all knew exactly where she was. Dana was glad to know that Chase was home with the other children.

After resting, Dana was sitting at the kitchen table trying to eat something. Tina walked toward the bathroom and stopped. She said, "Mom, I'm surprised, with all the problems that Armani's having, you haven't loss your mind."

Dana told her that she knows it's hard, but she was trying not to lose it.

Dana was back at the hospital again alone. Dana wished Pam was there with her. Dana didn't understand why Chase wasn't here with her. She knew he couldn't handle seeing her like this.

Armani's eyes were partially open. The nurse kept some kind of solution in them to keep them from drying out. She suctioned mucus from her every one to two hours, or when she sounded like she needs it. She would take a part of the respirator tube and suction her mouth; it pushed air in and came out. The nurse said it's a cough, but Dana can't really tell. It's like air that pushes out. Then she took a tube and put it in both of her nostrils one at a time to clear out what looked like mucus from a cold. It flew through the tube into a little jar. Right after they did the nose, they put that same tube into her mouth. It took the excess fluid that's sitting there inside the tube and then outside around the tube. Then she put the mouthpiece back before she suctioned her. She had to let the monitoring nurse know when she's doing this because it caused her heart rate to change.

Armani get three visitors, Dana's older sister and her two daughters, Ally and Clare. When Clare walked in, they were checking her heartbeat. There were a lot wires on her. Clare ran out. Dana ran after her and asked if she was okay. Clare said there were too many things on her. Dana told her, "Once they finish, all those wires will be off. Then she will appear a lot better to you with her Pampers and the blanket on her. Look, they're finished. Come on in."

They walked back in the room.

Dana smiled and said, "See, she looks much better now."

Clare said, "Wow! That was a lot of wires they had on her. I couldn't even see her."

Dana told her it's because she's so small.

Dana's sister Trudy, the oldest girl, always acted like she's the nurse of the family. Acted as though it was something she was used to. She stayed and watched everything. Then describe what was done, she said, "Oh, they just did this and that" to prove it didn't bother her. Dana called her Mrs. Nurse. She helped take care of all of their children. They would call her for medical advice; it always seemed to help. Dana was glad Trudy handled it well because her strength gave Dana strength.

Dana and her little sister Cindy had the same belief that if you cried, it meant you were giving up. Whenever

Dana felt like crying, she would fight to hold it in, which was very hard to do.

Ally went over to Armani and bent over to her and said, "Hey, little cousin, hurry up and get better." Armani's eye jumped a little. Ally was so excited. "She heard me!" she said. "Did you see that?" She was smiling as if it was a miracle.

Trudy and Clare smiled as well, hoping there was a breakthrough in Armani's condition. Another day went by, and Armani was still stable, and that was a good sign. Today was Sunday, and Dana forgot that she still hadn't called the insurance company yet, but first thing in the morning, she will.

It's now seven in the morning. Dana's sister Acee called, telling her she wanted to go with them to the hospital, so they had to wait for her. Acee promised to be at Dana's house by eight thirty in the morning to go to the hospital with her. Dana told her to please be there on time because she wanted to hurry up and get to the hospital. Acee was on time, but Chase wasn't ready yet. He was changing the message on the answering machine.

They did get out of the house on time. They parked in the parking lot as usual, which cost five dollars a day. The parking lot was packed that Monday morning because the clinic was open. This was a very busy hospital, but it was always clean. They took the elevator up to the room. Armani was still stable. Dana noticed that the back of Armani's neck had a dry patch on it because she was constantly lying on her back. Dana got some Vaseline and rubbed it on her neck. Chase didn't stay in the room long; he said it was only supposed to be two in a room, so he would wait in the waiting room. The waiting area didn't have a TV, only chairs, a bathroom, and a phone. That was the room Dana would stay in when she stayed all night.

Dana was outside of the waiting room talking to Ruth. Acee was inside the waiting room talking to Chase. Ruth and Dana heard Chase say that he felt like he's in jail when he had to stay in the hospital all day. He could not play with her or talk to her; he didn't like it at all. Ruth said her husband was the same way. That she would be the one at the hospital all the time. That was their way of handing it. Most men wouldn't or couldn't talk about or express their feelings. They have to be men and keep everything bottle all up inside. He would not go to the meeting with her. She would have to go alone, Ruth said, but that's the way men handled it. "So don't think he's being a bad husband. He is also a hurting husband and father."

Dana thanked her for helping her understand his way of dealing with Armani's illness. Acee stayed at the hospital all day with Dana and Chase. When they went for lunch, Acee didn't realize how expensive it was to spend a day at the hospital. So Chase ended up paying for her meal. After lunch, they were in the visitor room. Dana was eating some chips. Dana had developed an eating disorder. Her mother told her that her nerves have her eating so much. Ruth had told her that the same thing happened to her. Some people can't eat at all, but it was opposite for her and Dana; they ate like crazy.

Gloria and Mrs. Janie walked in. She smiled. "Hello, Dana, we came to see how you were doing, and you here stuffing your face."

Dana got up and hugged them and asked, "How did you know we were here?"

"We just came from seeing the baby, and the nurse told us."

Dana was in shock. "They let you in?"

Gloria said, "Only for a moment. The nurse said she couldn't let anyone in unless the mother or father is there, but I told her I was the godmother. Did anyone come up from the job yet?"

Dana said, "No, why?"

"Because the warden ordered someone from care and a priest to come up to give you some support."

Dana said, "Well, I've been here all day. I haven't seen anyone, and if I missed them, the nurse would have told me. Just like she is going to tell me that you were here."

Gloria grunted, "I don't believe this." She was right in her office when the warden gave the order for someone to report. She was so angry. "Well, I guess if the warden of the jail didn't get any respect, who will? This is some place we work at. Dana, we are going to leave. I have to take BJ for tutoring."

When they left, Chase went in the room, and Dana went with him. Dana said, "Look, Chase, she looks dirty. I'm going to bathe her.

Chase yelled, "You better not touch her with all those wires on her! You will get electrocuted."

Dana looked at him like he was crazy and yelled, "No, I won't."

He said, "You better let the nurse do it."

Dana looked at Armani with all those wires plugged into the wall. Dana figured he might be right, so she left her alone. She thought maybe he was afraid of her doing something wrong to her. That's why he said that to keep her from bathing her.

They finally left to go home. Tina had a job to do in Brooklyn as a movie extra, and Dana had to pick Pam up from Forty-Second Street. Pam would stay with Tina and her friend while Dana went to the hospital.

The next day, Dana, Tina, and her friend drove to Forty-Second Street. When they got there, Dana told them to go downstairs and that Pam would be sitting by the Greyhound station.

When they got out the car, Dana realized it was the wrong block. She jumped out of the van to try to stop them. They were nowhere in sight. Dana panicked, and she immediately parked the van in a parking lot. She quickly told the parking attendant she would only be fifteen minutes. Dana ran into port authority, found Pam, and said, "I just lost my child in Manhattan. Come on, I have to find them!"

They got in the van. Dana drove to the block she dropped them off at and jumped out. Dana told Pam to take the wheel. Dana said to just circle around. Pam yelled, "I might get lost!" but Dana kept walking nervously. She was sweating and scared and saying to herself, "Oh my god." She thought she needed to be with Armani and lost her older daughter out here. "Oh god, help me please." She ran across the street, running from corner to corner, then she didn't see Pam and the van. She thought see lost her too.

Dana walked back to check, and it turned out Pam had pulled over to the side. Pam told her that she will stay there until someone makes her move, then she will go around the block and back.

Dana went back to the port authority, walking through the crowd, and ran right into Tina and her friend, who was panicking too. Dana yelled, Thank god I found you! I'm sorry I let you off on the wrong block. I'm so glad you found port authority."

Tina said nervously, "We could not find Pam."

Dana told them, "Don't worry, I have her. Come on, let's go."

In the van, Dana was now relaxed. Pam told her, "Girl, you got a mess going on."

Dana exhaled and said, "I know." When Dana dropped them off at the school where the movie shoot was, she refused to leave them, so she stayed. Dana kept calling the hospital to check on Armani's condition, and she was still stable.

After the kids finished taping their movie scene, they went home and picked up Zeek from next door. Dana took Tina and Zeek home and dropped off Pam's bags.

Pam and Dana went to the hospital. It was a different nurse from the usual one. She was very relaxed but nice. Dana said to Pam, "Armani looks dirty." She wished Sally was in. She would have bathed her and lotioned her down.

Armani was covered with her pink blanket, and her pink teddy bear that Tina bought her for Christmas lay next to her. Pam told Dana to bathe her. Dana told her that she didn't think she could. Pam asked why. Dana told that Chase told her that she or Armani can get electrocuted if she did.

Pam said, "I never heard nothing like that." Pam said asked the nurse when she came back in the room.

Dana asked, "Can she get a bath?"

The nurse replied, "Yes, sure she can, if you like." The nurse walked out the room to get some soap, a pan of water, and a washcloth. She put everything on the table. While dipping the cloth in the water, she watched the TV that Acee and Dana had put on Monday. She dipped the cloth in the water again. She asked, "Do you want to do it or me?"

Dana said, "I thought you had to do it."

The nurse said, "No, you can."

Pam blurted out, "She scared because her husband told her that she can get electrocuted if she bathe her."

The nurse busted out laughing and assured her that it's not true. "I'll do it."

They all laughed. The nurse gave her a nice bath and lotioned her all over. Dana changed her socks and her blanket. When they were getting ready to leave, Pam gave Armani a kiss on her hand and on her forehead and touched her Pampers.

Dana said, "What did you do, kiss her Pampers?"

The nurse started laughing again and said, "You two are funny."

They all laughed. Pam tried to explain what happened. She said she kissed her hand and her forehead, than touched her Pampers.

The nurse said, "One getting electrocuted, the other one kissing her Pampers. Wow, what a laugh."

They laughed all the way home.

The next day, Dana called her job health center. She was upset, trying to speak to someone about what was going on. As she tried to tell him, she started crying. The person she was talking to was afraid Dana was going to hurt herself. He asked her did she have a weapon. He made an appointment for her to come in that morning.

Before Dana left, she made a concept tape for Zeek to talk to Armani since he couldn't go up to see her. The nurse said it would be fine since Armani can hear them. Dana asked Zeek what he wanted to say to Armani, and he said he wanted to sing something. Dana turned the recorder on, and Zeek began to sing. "I'm a little Armani…short and strong…here is my hand, and here is my mouth. When I get all hungry you hear me shout… just pick up a bottle and put it in my mouth. I love you, Armani, I miss you. Come home soon."

Then Tina made a message also for Armani because she couldn't handle seeing Armani like that. Tina said, "Hi, moo-moo, I miss you! Hope to see you soon."

Dana also put Armani's favorite song on the tape, "Only for a While." Then Dana packed up the tape and player put it in a black bag. She then dropped the kids at school. Dana and Pam drove to pick up Dee so Pam could stay with her at her job while Dana went to the health office. Pam stayed with Dee since she worked right next door in the same building.

Chapter

FOURTEEN

In the health office, speaking to one of their assigned psychiatrists, Dana could hardly speak. Tears were falling like a rain. She tried to explain what was going on with Armani and how bad she needed to be with her and not there. Dana tried to explain that Armani was on a respirator and cried. He passed her a few tissues. She told him how stressed she was not able to sleep. He looked at her as though he's speechless. He rushed out of the room to tell the captain he needed to put her out of work. Then he returned. He looked down at his paperwork and began to fill it out. He told her there is nothing he can do for her, except talk about it. Dana told him she joined Big Heart Little Heart. He suggested she continue to go. He was really no help. Dana left to sign out with the captain.

They put her out sick for eight days with twenty-four hours out the house and were told after the eight days, she would have 1:00 p.m. to 5:00 p.m. recreation hours out of the house. After the eight days, she had to fax a letter over to the main office for more hours out the house. They ordered her to change her ID to no weapon. She was not allowed to carry her weapon, which she had to keep locked in the control room.

This was time Dana could have spent with her baby. She had to be in Manhattan to change her ID. Dana did all of this in one day. Then she rushed back to the hospital.

Pam was her extra head; she reminded Dana of the things she had to do so Dana could keep her mind on Armani and the kids at home.

One day, Zeek said somebody ate all the food. Dana forgot to shop for the house.

At the hospital, Dana plugged in the tape player and played the tape. Nurse Jenny said, "Oh my god, it's so sad." She had to leave as she started to cry after she heard Zeek's song and his message. She didn't come back until the tape finished.

Dana also brought a picture of Zeek and Tina with Armani and hung it up on the edge of her bed, along with a picture of just Armani next to it. In the picture Armani, had a look as if she was asking, "What are you doing to me?"

That was a long day for Dana and Pam. They watched the nurse suction her and change her lines. They planned to do catheterization on her the next day, so a couple of doctors came in to explain. Dr. Rice explained what he was going to do, how the procedure was going to be handled. He said they already had a line in her thigh, so that's the line they were going to use to insert the catheter. He would use a balloon to try and open up her clogged artery.

Dana and Pam left around nine that night to make sure they got enough sleep. They wanted to make it there in time for the procedure.

The next morning, they were running a little late, and they got there around nine thirty. They were getting ready to take her in early because there was a cancellation. Dana was glad she made it there in time so she could give Armani a little talk. "Armani, this is Mommy. You have to be strong to make it through this, okay? Mommy and Daddy loves you. Zeek and Tina too."

Pam cut in. "And your cousin Pam. We all love you."

Dana said, "That's right, moo-moo." She sang a little song to her. "Oooh, oooh, when you cry...I'll always pick you up...hold you tight to keep you safe and warm. Sing to you, I'll sing your favorite song...to watch your smile...oh that precious smile..." Then she said, "Okay, little one. Be strong. Mommy will be waiting right here for you. Love you." Then Dana gave her a big kiss on her forehead and then on her hand. Pam was already kissing her other hand.

The nurses and doctors walked in and start switching things over to smaller equipment so Armani could be moved safely. When the respirator was removed, a big bottle was used to suction her to keep her breathing going. Sometimes she would override the respirator and breathe on her own. But they kept her on it; they didn't want to take any chance on losing her.

It took eleven staff members to move her. Dana and Pam followed them to the elevator, but it was too full, so the nurse told them to wait in the visitor rest room, and she will come and get them as soon as it was over. The procedure takes about four to five hours.

Dana wiped away her tears and went to do what she did best during stressed—eat in the cafeteria. Chase would call the hospital every morning and evening to check on Armani's condition. He would speak to the nurse if Dana wasn't around. It was really hard for him.

Finally the procedure was over. Dr. Peterson came in and told them that the procedure was done, but they were unable to open up the clogged artery. He said they used the biggest balloon they had, and it didn't clear it. Dr. Peterson said after they get their report together, and they would have another meeting. They were going to send what they had to a hospital in New York for their opinion.

Before Dana went downstairs for the meeting, she had a talk with Ruth. Ruth tried to get Dana prepared for what was going to be done. Dana cried, wiping away her tears, forcing to keep them in her, not giving up. Ruth told her that she understands, and that was also how she felt when her little girl had her surgery.

Pam went with Dana to the meeting. Nurse Jill was there. The doctor explained that one of the holes in her heart had closed. He said it's like the valve was not even there; blood was just gushing through. He thought the best thing to do was to replace the valve and do a bypass, freezing the heart. Doing the bypass, they would open up that clogged artery. Armani would have to take a blood thinner for the rest of her life. He made Dana feel very confident in what he was going to do.

When they walked out of the office, Pam sped past Dana and went around a corner. Dana followed Pam, and when she found her, Pam had broken down in tears. Dana walked away and let her be until she got herself together. She didn't want Pam's tears to weaken her faith that Armani was going be okay.

When Pam finally got herself together, she came back. Dana asked her if she was okay.

Pam said, "Yes, my god, you never really know what's going on until you speak to the doctors."

Dana said, "I know. Remember when Dr. Carp spoke to us earlier? He broke it down, he said…he said it's a risky operation. She might not survive it, and then he walked out."

Dana thought he was unconfident. Dr. Peterson at least made her feel it could work. Dana liked that feeling as it restored her strength that it's going to be fine.

The next day, Acee came over early again to spend time at the hospital with Dana and Pam. On their way, they stopped at a bookstore. Pam bought two bibles, one for Armani and the other for her. They sat with Armani reading the Bible all day, different scriptures. Dana cleaned Armani's earrings with alcohol on a Q-tip. She greased her dry skin with lotion and changed her socks. She sat her teddy bear next to her and played with her hand. Armani's hand was so chubby; they would wrap around Dana's finger. Her hand held on to her the wonderful feeling of life from this sedated child who couldn't move or cry, who was being fed some white minerals through a tube, along with loads of medication.

Dana was frightened by the effect the medication would do to her. The nurse told her that they took a blood test every day to test her liver and lungs, also to make sure no side effects were taking place. They had to put a pint of blood in her to replace what they had taken from her. Dana was concerned after the surgery as they planned to give her morphine. The nurse told her that she was going to be addicted just like an addict, and that's why they were going to wean her off with methadone. She told Dana most mothers didn't want their kids to have morphine, but when they see the pain they go through, they change their minds.

Dana's face had a look of pain and asked, "How do the children turn out once they're off it? Are they normal?"

The nurse just looked at her.

Dana sighed. "Oh boy, I will be glad when this is over."

Pam moaned, "Me too, it's too much. Our heart is crying in pain. It hurts seeing her like this."

Dana said, "She's so tiny and innocent. How can a little baby take so much? She is strong and fighting from day one." Dana looked around the room. "Where is Acee?"

Pam told her she's in the waiting room. "I think she's ready to go."

Dana asked what time it was.

Pam looked at the clock. "It's eight thirty."

Dana said, "Yeah, I guess it's time to take her home."

They started to pack up.

Dana said, "Maybe we can get to see Zeek before he goes to sleep. He will enjoy that." Dana told the nurse they were getting ready to go and that she will call back at two in the morning to see how she's doing.

The nurse said, "I'll be right here."

Another night at home, and Dana tried to get a good night's sleep. The phone rang. It's Jill calling to see how the baby was doing. The phone kept cutting off. Jill called back and asked Dana, "What's wrong with your phone?"

Dana replied, "I don't know, it keeps cutting off."

Jill said, "You better get—"

The phone cut off.

Dana yelled frantically, "Hello? Hello! Oh god, what is wrong with this phone?"

The phone rang again.

"Hello, yeah, Dana? This is a bad time for your phone to be acting up."

Dana yelled to her that she knew and that she was going to call.

The phone cut off again.

"Hello, hello! Damn, this can't be happening!" Dana shouted.

Pam asked what it was doing. Dana described that it got a lot of static, and then it cut off. The phone rang again. Dana picked up the phone. "Oh god, hello!" Dana yelled.

Jill said, "Yeah, Dana, you better hurry up and get it checked out. You want the hospital to be able to get in touch with you."

Dana yelled, "I know, let me—"

The phone cut off again.

Dana yelled, "Hello! Hello! Hello! Damn!"

The phone rang again. Dana yelled to Pam, "I wish she would stop calling me back so I could get it fixed." She picked up the phone. "Hello, yeah, Jill, I'm—hello! Hello!

Ah, man." Dana hung up the phone, put on some clothes, and ran next door to call the phone company.

Dana banged on the door, and Keisha opened the door. Dana yelled quickly while trying to catch her breath, "Keisha, is it okay if I can make a phone call to the phone company? My phone is acting up."

Keisha said yes.

Dana ran to the phone, picked it up, and called the phone company. "Hello, yes, I'm having trouble with my phone. The number is... Do I have a cordless phone? Yes."

They told Dana to unplug it for a while because sometime the cordless phone knocked out the other lines. Dana ran home and tried it, but it didn't work. Dana went back to call the phone company and told them it didn't work. She said, "Listen, I have a baby in the hospital on a respirator. I need my phone working in case the hospital needs to get in touch with me! She demanded that she needed her phone working now.

The lady said she was sorry to hear that, and she will get somebody out as soon as possible. "But if the problem is in your line inside, you're going to have to pay."

Dana told her it was no problem and hung up. Then she called the hospital and told Nurse Janie that her phone was not working. So if she needed to get in touch with her to take down a number to reach her. The nurse asked will they give her the message, and Dana said, "Yes they related the message to me." Dana gave her the phone number then hung up and went back next door.

That night, Dana could not relax. Dana walked around all night and couldn't sleep. Two in the morning, Dana called the neighbor to let her know that the hospital might call because she wasn't home when she went by earlier. Wilma told her not to worry.

Dana lay down and tried to get some sleep. She suddenly realized that she had a cell phone that stayed in her pocketbook because she couldn't use it in the hospital. She plugged it up to charge it. Then she went in the room where Pam was sleeping and told her, Do you know I could have used my cell phone?"

Pam told Dana, "You got a lot on your mind. You wasn't thinking."

Dana picked up the cell phone and called the hospital and gave Nurse Janie the number. The nurse took down the number, then she told Dana that Armani was still in stable condition, and she urged Dana to relax and get some rest.

Dana could rest a little better now that she had a working phone.

At eight in the morning, the telephone man showed up to repair the phone.

Chapter

FIFTEEN

Sunday morning, Dana, Chase, and Pam went to the hospital. Dr. Boxx was there, and he told them that Armani was scheduled for surgery Tuesday. Dana was surprised and said, "She is?"

The doctor replied, "Yes, she is. It's really risky. We sent the report to the New York hospital. It's either change the valve that has the leakage or a heart transplant. There is so much going on with her heart. The heart muscle is weak."

Dana and Chase both were against the transplant. They knew she could be on a waiting list too long, and the thought of waiting for someone to die to get their heart was upsetting. Chase asked him what did he think would be best.

Dr. Boxx said, "Well, a heart transplant is a very risky operation. She'll be in and out of hospitals. We would have to watch her carefully, and it's not a guarantee the heart will take. Most of all, you're right, the waiting for a heart. I think we should try to change the valve because she can't stay on a respirator too long. Listen, Dr. Peterson is going to meet with you on Monday and explain the operation to you. I will be around if you have any questions. Okay?" Dr. Boxx soon left.

Dana said, "Honey, what do you think about this?"

Chase, with a disgraced look on his face, said, "Well, I know something has to be done, and it has to be done soon."

Dana replied, "I know, but, Chase, he's talking about a heart transplant now."

Chase yelled, "No! No way, no heart transplant. We're just gonna let them change the valve."

Dana agreed that would be best.

Armani had some more visitors. Dana's mother and her sister Cindy and Cindy's husband Ramon came in. Dana's mother Adele asked, "When is the surgery?"

Dana told her it's scheduled for Tuesday morning.

Ramon asked, "Whose Bible is this?"

"That's Armani's Bible," Dana responded.

He picked it up and started to read scripture to scripture out loud. As he read them, he marked them so that Dana could find them later. Dana's mother Adele yelled out one of her favorite ones for him to find and read. It almost felt like they were in a church, until the nurse came in and said visiting time was up. As long as it was three of them in the room, they never said anything. This day it must have been too many visitors in the room.

They all left, and everyone bid Armani bye. She was heavily sedated the whole time. Her eyes almost opened, lying on her side from when the nurse switched her. They moved her every once in a while to keep her from getting bed sores.

All of her family and friends were all praying, keeping her on the prayer list at each of their churches in Brooklyn, Queens, Long Island, and Boston, and whoever knew her. Dana wondered if anyone was listening to her or heard her calls. Dana would always pray to God to please take her pain away and give her strength.

On Monday, Dana and Chase and Pam were in Armani's room. Nurse Jane came in and said, "Good morning, Mr. and Mrs. Frazier. I have some good news and bad news. Actually, it's good news for her. They postponed the surgery to Thursday. The reason is so that we can wean her off of the heart medication. It's the strongest heart medication that adults would take. They believe if they don't get her off it, she won't survive the surgery. She might not pull through the bypass, so it's safer for her, and it's bad for you because I know you want to get the surgery over with and have her safe back in your arms. Believe me, it's better that we make it safe for her. It's a difficult operation. We just don't want anything to go wrong."

Chase said, "Well, we want what's best for her also. So we just have to wait."

"Okay. Dr. Peterson is going to have another meeting with both of you since Mr. Frazier wasn't able to make it Friday. He's going to go through it again for you. So I'll be back up around two to take you down for the meeting. Any questions you have to ask, write them down so that you won't forget them. Okay. Well, I'll be back around two." She turned to leave.

Dana sighed in frustration. "Oh man, this is driving me crazy. It just doesn't get any better. What happens once they take her off the medication? What if her heart can't take it?"

Pam yelled, "Write it down, write it down!"

Dana said, "Yeah, give me a piece a paper." Dana started to write and think about what other questions she wanted to ask.

Pam said, "How about the blood thinner? Remember, you said if she gets hurt, could she bleed to death?"

"Yes," Dana said, "that's a good question."

For some reason, they could not think of anything else to ask. But Dana kept the pen and paper in her hand in case they thought of any more questions.

At two in the afternoon, they went downstairs for the meeting. Pam decided to stay in New York longer for support since they had changed the surgery. She called her job for more time off while they were in the meeting.

Dr. Peterson was a very nice man. He explained the surgery all over again for Chase. Chase asked him what the valve looked like. Dana though, *Wow, that was a good question.* Dr. Peterson went and got it to show them what the valve looked like. It was a round black hard piece of plastic the size of a nickel. There were two flaps; one opened and one closed one way. On one side felt like a hard thread around the edge of it.

Dana asked, "This is going in her little heart?"

He said yes. They asked him questions, and he answered. Dana asks about the burns on her chest. He told her that those burns on her chest were from the electric shocks from that Friday night, March 13. They had to shock her twenty times that night. That is the reason they inserted the pacemaker, to keep her alive, and that's why they couldn't use the electric shock anymore. The blood thinner would be taken the rest of her life, and it could cause uncontrollable bleeding because the blood would not clot that easily if she cut herself.

They felt confident in him. He didn't sound as if he was afraid to do the surgery. He was very confident and in control. Chase and Dana had a thing with that if you sound afraid, they didn't want them to do it.

Dana and Chase finally asked about the heart medicine that they were weaning her off of. They asked him what if her heart couldn't take it. Dr. Peterson said being that her heart muscle was weak, it's a chance they had to take. But they were not going to take her off it altogether but to lower it. If they can get her to the lowest without causing a risk to her life, that would be good.

That meeting with Dr. Peterson made Dana wonder if she should approach Chase about that question no one wanted to bring up. When she finally had enough courage, Dana asked Chase, "What if something happens? What are we going to do?"

Chase replied, "There's no need to even discuss anything like that. Just have faith, think positive."

Dana felt a little bad for even thinking the worst. They went back to Armani's room. She had a one on one. That's like a training nurse's aide. She sat with patience. She was slim with dark skin and wild curly hair. Her wig was not a very well-kept wig. She had a very strong Southern voice, but she didn't say much, just watched the monitors. Chase kissed Armani good night to and went home to be with the other kids.

Pam was very sociable. Pam asked the aide a question and couldn't resist her Southern accent. "Do you mind if I ask where you're from?"

She said, "I was born in Bensenville, South Carolina."

Pam said, "Oh really? I have family that's from North Carolina."

The aide asked, "What's your last name?"

They both went back and forth, trying to connect the two families to see what family married into what family. It appeared that most of the times, family end up marrying a third or fourth they didn't know about. When they found out they're related, the marriage ends up breaking up.

Both women get into a conversation about living in the South, growing up using the outhouse, the snakes, and the good old whipping with the tree twigs. The respect children gave the adults: yes, sir; no, sir.

Dana was really surprised by some of the things Pam went through. It really shocked Dana when Pam talked about her grandmother. Dana always felt a little jealous because she never met her mother's mom. Pam's and Dana's parents were brother and sister. Dana's mother moved to New York, and that's where Dana was born and raised. Dana had to wait till she was older and working to pay for her own ticket to travel to the north, but by then her grandmother had already passed away, but she did meet her grandfather.

They went on and on until the head nurse started to change Armani's lines and cleaned her up. Another nurse came in who was black and heavyset.

Dana remembered that horrible night when Armani first came in the hospital On Friday the thirteenth. She complained about the nurse who called to tell Dana to come back to the hospital, that Armani took a turn for the worse. She fussed. No, she wasn't supposed to do that. "You could have killed yourself trying to get here."

Dana said, "You're right." If Gloria was there to drive her, she would have been in trouble.

The nurse was still complaining while putting on her gloves. The aide put on gloves too to help. All three were busy changing her. Nurse Linda put down the railing on the bed. Dana ran over to kiss Armani to get a nice easy kiss without standing on her tiptoes, bending over trying to kiss her. Dana kissed Armani's face all over; she missed that.

It got so busy that Dana and Pam decided to leave so the nurses could continue without them getting in the way. They had machines all over the place. There was actually too many of them in the room.

Dana packed up, and she and Pam left feeling good that Armani was getting 105 percent treatment.

Chapter

SIXTEEN

The next morning, Dana and Pam walked into the room. There was a little white girl with straight blonde hair. She was with her mother and a nurse in the room.

Dana screamed as she ran out of the room, "Where is my baby?" Her heart raced a mile a minute.

A nurse from behind the desk came running to her. "Mrs. Frazier, she's okay. We just moved her to another room. She's no longer isolated." She directed Dana to a bigger room. In the room was another baby with her mother in there. Pam and Dana walked in. They didn't like the room.

They both walked over to check on Armani. She was sitting up in some sort of position. Dana didn't like it. She looked uncomfortable. Dana moved her around a little to make her comfortable. Pam asked how come they took her from the other room. "It looks like they changed the tape from around her mouth."

Dana was upset that they put Armani in there. Dana said, "Last night they were changing her lines and everything, seems like she was getting a royal treatment, and then they kick her out to the wolves."

When the nurse came in, Dana asked her why Armani was in isolation. She said, "Well, she had the flu, so there are no signs of it, it's all cleared up."

Dana asked, "Why is she lying with her head raised up like this?"

"Well, the head nurse, Sandy, on the early shift sat her up like that because she was sounding congested."

Dana didn't argue because she knew how it sounded when she heard that sound, which used to be from the leakage. That's one reason they increase the medication. Dana asked if it was okay if she made her look a little more comfortable to her.

The nurse said, "Sure, you're her mother. You can question anyone on her behavior."

Dana moved Armani in a position that made her feel comfortable.

The baby in the room had a visitor there with the mother. Pam went out to call her job to tell them she was going to stay out another week. Dana stayed in the room when she heard the visitor ask the baby's mother what happened to Armani. The mother told her she didn't know. Dana just grabbed Armani's hand and put her head down. Dana never had to deal with the public since Armani's been in that condition. She's always been in a private room. *Isolation room*, Dana thought. Dana didn't have to face anyone but the medical staff who already knew Armani's condition. Dana didn't know how to explain to anyone, if they asked, what was going on with her little baby with all this medication that's being pumped into her.

A young man was cleaning the television. Armani's television was next to be cleaned. He moved the ladder over to Armani's side and started cleaning the TV. Dana asked him if she should move. He said, "No, it's okay." Then he did it. He asked with his Spanish accent, "What happen to the baby?"

Dana said she had a heart failure. Dana didn't know where that answer came from, but it just came out.

"Oh god," he said. "I hope she'll be okay."

Dana just thanked him.

He continued to speak. "That's why I don't want any kids right now. You never know if something goes wrong. That's what I told my girlfriend. She got pregnant twice already. I told her to get rid of them, but she wants to have one."

"Well, how old are you?" Dana asked.

He answered, "I'm twenty three, and she's seventeen."

"Oh no," Dana said. "Tell her to concentrate on school."

He said, "I know, that's what I keep trying to tell her, but she won't listen." He finished up and climb down from the ladder. "Okay, I hope she feels better." Then he left.

Dana was hoping Pam hurry back so she can help her answer that question people would ask her. When Dana heard the lady ask the baby's mother what happened to Armani, Dana didn't respond because she didn't want to go into details.

When Pam came back into the room, Dana told Pam that she was glad she was back. She hated it when someone asked her what happened to the baby. It was hard for her to go into details with them and see the look on their faces. The look of sadness and hurt was, for her, so painful to deal with.

The nurse returned with a female doctor. They told Dana that she needed to switch Armani's lines so that all the medication went through to the other side. If it stayed on that one side too long, it could get infected. The doctor explained that it was a very sterile procedure and that Dana and Pam would have to leave.

Dana said, "So we have to leave? What about the lady and her baby?"

The nurse told her that everything was fully covered and protected; it has to be totally sterile. They had moved the mother and her baby out as well.

Dana took a deep breath and watched as they brought the machines in fully covered. Dana told Pam, "Let's go, I don't want them to ask me to leave again." Of course Dana was upset. They went to the cafeteria for lunch. By the time Pam and Dana returned back from lunch, the procedure was finished. All the lines were put in the left leg, but the other lines had not been removed yet from the right leg. The nurse was getting ready to change them when Nurse Sally told her to wait until this evening when she had to change all the tubes. This was changed every night.

The evening shift started, and the nurse had started to change the tubes; she looked frustrated like too much was going on. Maybe she was disturbed by the mother carefully watching her. Dana told her they were going to go for dinner, and hopefully by the time they get back, she'll be finished.

By the time Dana and Pam got back, the nurse still was changing the lines. She asked Dana if she could give her a little more time. Dana said okay, but she wanted her to know she didn't like this. Dana only left because she didn't want her to make any mistakes.

Dana walked back out and went downstairs to call Tina. When she got back upstairs, Dana told Tina to call her back. Dana told Pam to wait for Tina to call her back. She was going to check on Armani. When she went up to her room, Dana could see right inside her room before entering. There were about fifty doctors and nurses and aides in the room. Dana yelled to Pam that something was going wrong. Pam didn't hear Dana. Dana couldn't wait anymore.

Dana went running in Armani's room. One aide saw her and came to stop her. Dana stopped and stared at them. The aide asked her if she wanted a chair. Another nurse yelled that she shouldn't be in here and walked away. The aide asked Dana again, "Do you want a chair?" She didn't dare ask her to leave.

Dana looked in the room. She saw a young doctor hold the electric shock to Armani's chest. Dana yelled, "Oh god!" Now she knew what was going on. Her whole body began to shake. Tears started running down her face. She wiped them away because Dana knew she was going to be alright. Dana refused to give up on her faith. Dana prayed to herself. *Oh god, stop the pain please. Stop the pain!* Her heart was hurting so bad, and now it was beating so loud and so hard. Dana just wanted to drop were she stood and beg for help.

Nurse Jane came in. "Mrs. Frazier, you shouldn't be here and watching this. Come." She motioned for Dana to follow her.

Dana went to the door and stood there. The nurse asked Dana, "Where's your friend?" Dana told her she's at the phone. Nurse Jane walked Dana over around the corner to get Pam. Nurse Jane said to Pam, "Keep her out here." Pam had no idea that something was going on. She was on the phone with Tina. Dana heard her tell Tina to put Chase on the phone.

"What's wrong?" Tina asked.

"Nothing," Pam said, "just put Chase on the phone."

Once Chase got on the phone, she told him to get to the hospital right away. She quickly hung up.

"Pam, I have to go back there."

"Dana, you can't stand there. Please, Dana, stay over here," Pam pleaded with her. "Alright, Dana, let's just stand outside the door."

When they go over to Armani's room, the outside door is closed. Also the lady whose baby that was in the room with Armani was out in the hallway too. The nurse came out and asked Dana if she wanted a chair. Dana didn't answer, but she brought a chair out to her anyway. Dana sat down nervously and was shaking knowing that her other half was inside that room with about fifty or so medical staff trying to help her.

Nurse Jane came out and told Dana, "Dr. Boxx is here. Her blood pressure is stable." Then she went back in the room.

Then a few minutes later, Dr. Coop came out, and he said, "Her blood pressure is down, and it doesn't look good. And he walked back in the room.

Dana couldn't stand him. She turned her head to hold back her tears. The mother of Armani's roommate came over and put both her hands on Dana's hands on both sides of the chair. "Go ahead and cry. Go ahead, let it out." She started shaking the chair until Dana yelled at her. No, she can't cry! She's not giving up on her. "She's going to be—"

The lady cut her off. "Yes, she is going to be fine."

Dana burst out with a really loud cry, but still she tried to hold it in. Dana saw a priest walk by, and Nurse Jane came out.

Dana yelled, "What is he doing here?" Dana thought they had given up on Armani already. Nurse Jane assured her that the priest was there for another family who was having a crisis. In the meanwhile, Dana wasn't aware that Pam asked Jane to stay with Dana while Pam made a call. Pam called the house to see if Chase had left.

When Pam returned, Chase was there. Chase walked up to Dana. Nurse Jane must have forgotten how he looked because as he walked up, she asked Dana, "Do you know this man?"

Dana looked at her and said, "Yes, that's my husband."

"Oh," she said. "Mr. Frazier, I tried to get your wife to go to the office so everyone doesn't know your business." At this time the nurse's aide is in the process of closing up the area. She closed the door to the entrance and posted a sign that said to use back entrance. Dana knew this didn't look good at all. She could no longer see the room.

Nurse Jane escorted Dana, Chase, and Pam to Dr. Boxx's office. Jane said that everybody who could help her now was in the room with her now. Jane left the office. Then she came back and said the priest had seen what was going on and asked if he could baptize Armani. Dana and Chase both said yes. She left. When Nurse Jane came back, she said that the baptism went beautifully.

The door opened again, and Dr. Boxx and Dr. Coop both came in together. Dana couldn't hear the words he was saying, but she felt the pain in her heart as he motioned. He said, "I'm sorry, we did everything we could have done, but we lost her."

Dana turned to Pam, who was behind her. Dana began punching her, trying to beat the pain away. Her knees just weakened, and Dana gave in and fell to the floor. Pam and Nurse Jane tried to hold her. Pam got lost in the midst of it all and began to break out in tears. Nurse Jane yelled at her, "You have to be strong for her! Help me take her to the couch in the room."

Dana felt like she was floating to the room as they placed her on the couch. Dana fell to the floor and began beating it over and over. Someone was passing her tissue and water. All Dana remembered seeing were those shiny shoes sitting next to her. Dana was so lost. Then Pam got down on the floor with her. She grabbed her and held her. Then Dana let go and pushed her away. Dana just wanted to beat something.

The priest came in. Dana didn't know what he was saying; it didn't register. Dana ripped the tissue into pieces and threw it. Dana couldn't believe this was happening. This had to be a dream. It couldn't be real.

Chase came in from seeing Armani when the doctor told him they lost her. Chase demanded to see her. When he came back in the room with Dana, he asked for some privacy. As everyone left, he held Dana and burst out with a loud cry.

Pam went to make some calls. First she called Cindy, Dana's sister, but she wasn't home. Her husband, Ramon, answered the phone. Pam asked if Cindy was home, and he said, "No, she's at work." Pam told him they just lost Armani. He said, "Oh no." Pam told him to let Cindy know. Then she decided to call Adele, Dana's mother. When she did, Adele picked up the phone, and Pam asked her what was Rob's number and that she wanted to ask him something. She told Adele she misplace his number. Pam thought Adele already knew something was wrong. Adele gave Pam the number, and Pam said thanks and hung up.

Pam called Rob, but Dee picked up. Pam asked, "Is Rob home?"

Dee asked, "What's wrong?" Pam asked her if she's home alone. "No." Dee asked again, "What's wrong?"

Pam told her, "We just lost Armani."

She said, "Oh no" and called Rob to the phone. Pam told him she got his number from Aunt Adele, but didn't tell her what was going on because of her condition. He said okay and wanted to know what time they would be home. Pam told him around eight or eight thirty. Then Pam hung up the phone.

Nurse Sally walked in. "Mrs. Frazier, we're getting ready to clean her up. Do you want to help?"

Chase said, "I don't think she's ready."

Dana jumped up and said yes. Dana just had to see her baby for the last time.

Nurse Sally put her arm around Dana's shoulders as they walked. She told Dana she put up a fight. She fought for a whole hour.

When they got in the room, Armani was lying there. She still had the lines in her thigh. Sally passed Dana the baby oil, but Dana couldn't do it, so Sally did it. She asked Dana if she wanted to hold her. Dana said yes, and she sat in this big chair in the room. Nurse Sally picked Armani up and put her in Dana's arms.

It was so nice to see her face without that tube in her mouth. She was so warm. Dana rubbed her face and kissed her all over. Chase was holding her hand.

Dr. Boxx came in. "Do you want your friend to come in?"

Dana thought Pam would want to see her, and Dana said yes. Pam walked in and looked at Dana holding this deceased baby. She had this look on her face as if to say, "Is she crazy?" Pam started crying with fear. Dana just waved her hand at her to get out and go. Dana continued to kiss Armani. Chase asked if he could hold her. Armani was so heavy and lifeless as Dana put her in Chase's arms. Dana held the back of her head. But her neck was sinking down, and he had to adjust his arm to hold her straight. Once he had her, he kissed her face. Dana kissed her hand. Dana told the doctor she was still warm.

He said he knew. He wanted to know if they wanted an autopsy to be done. Dana and Chase both agreed that she been through so much, and they said no. Chase held her until the warmth of her body was almost gone. They put her back in the bed. There was someone there taking pictures. Dana put her pink blanket on her and put her pink teddy bear by her face. She still had on her earrings. The mole in her head was starting to sink in.

They left after Dana packed up all of her belongings. Her black bag with the tape recorder, socks, Bible, blankets, and teddy bear, along with hat and the pictures that were by her bed. Chase shook Dr. Boxx's hand. Dana shook his hand, but felt some sort of closeness to him. He was the last hand to touch Armani alive. Dana pulled him to her and gave him a big hug. He hugged her back. Dana hugged Nurse Jane too and thanked her for hanging in there with them.

While leaving on the way out of the hospital, Dana realized there was no need for her to come back there anymore. Dana bust out crying. Chase held her, and he asked her if she wanted to stop. Dana said no, so they kept walking. Chase drove his car. Pam drove the van back to the house, while Dana sat in the van, still in shock of her loss.

When they got home, Dana went to her room and took off her clothes and put on her pajamas. She lay down on her bed. Tina came down and went to the bathroom. Dana got up and went into the bathroom with her. Dana told Tina, "We lost Armani."

Tina burst out in tears. Dana held her for a good while, and then Dana went back to bed. Rob and Dee stopped by, then Gloria, Cindy, her mother Adele, and Ramon came over too. Dana got up, went into the living room, and sat for a few minutes. Then she got up and went into the kitchen. She started to look around and saw Armani's medication. She picked it up and started throwing it away. She went into the refrigerator and took the medication from there and threw it away. She picked up her pacifier, stopped, looked at it, and put it back. Dana couldn't throw it away. It had a smell of her milky saliva. It was too connected to her, so she put it back on the counter and got back in her bed. Her head was hurting her so bad.

Her heart was crying, and so were many others hearts crying for little Armani. She will be missed in so many ways. Her four-year-old brother who still asked for her or spoke her name of things he remembers. Her seventeen-year-old sister, who gave Armani her nickname and middle name and loved listening to her trying to sing.

Dana could not bear the pain in her heart. Dana left the pacifier on the counter for days, weeks, then months. Dana could not bear to prepare for the funeral. Chase got Acee and Gloria to help him. He knew it was something that had to be done. So he searched for the insurance policies and headed to a funeral home. What did he know about New York when he was born and raised in Boston? Chase found a place near the house. Later, the funeral home called him back on the house phone to tell him that the cemetery he chose will not accept Armani because she was too big. Chase was furious.

The funeral director tried to keep him calm. Chase got louder, fussing that they dare deny his child. Dana overheard the conversation and knew she had to take over. When the funeral director called back, Dana picked up the phone and talked to her.

Chase, Dana, and Acee drove to the burial site to check it out. This cemetery will accept her. This cemetery had a day care center and a playground right in the cemetery. Chase was fussing. He didn't think it was a good resting place with the activities around. Dana felt it was just right for Armani. She calmly explained what it felt like to her. She said, "It's different, it's not like visiting a regular cemetery where there is no noise, nothing going on." She felt at ease with Armani being there, that there will be children around her playing. Dana said when they come to visit, the sounds of the children laughing and playing would keep Armani company.

Eventually Chase did understand and respected Dana's wishes.

Chapter

SEVENTEEN

A t the funeral, Dana went to view Armani's body. She was dressed in a white satin dress with a matching hat, and her three favorite stuffed animals were nicely placed beside her. Dana burst out in tears with Chase at her side to sweep her up from falling to the floor. The funeral director, Dana's devoted pastor, and a pastor who was sent from Dana's job spoke at the service. Also Dana's brother Rob said a few kind words about his niece that he only knew for five months. When the funeral director asked if anyone else wanted to speak, Zeek put his hand up, but the funeral director did not see him. Beatrice did not show up. Dana was hoping that she would walk in and speak.

Back at the house, Mary walked in with a bunch of food she just cooked. She had buffalo wings, barbecue turkey wings, tossed salad, pasta salad, rice and beans, eggplant parmesan, potato salad, and cake. She placed it all on the kitchen table. Someone brought some fried chicken. Trudy made rice and beans also. Mary was mad because some of Dana's family packed up food and took it home. Mary said she made that food for the house for the family. Dana was upset, but not too upset about the food when she just buried her daughter. That was hard enough for her to digest.

Healing for Dana wasn't easy. Her job locked her in the house right after the funeral. She was only allowed out the house from one to five in the afternoon, four hours a day. Pam left soon after the funeral, Chase went back to Boston, and the kids returned to school. When Dana asked for more time out the house, she was rudely denied.

Dana requested to go to her job health department to see the psychiatrist to put her back to work. When she did go to see him, he didn't think that Dana was able to talk about what happened without uncontrollable crying. Dana begged him to send her back while wiping away her tears. She told him she needed to get her head together, and the house along with things that reminded her of Armani wasn't helping her. He would not send her back to work.

Bills were coming in addressed to Armani; Dana would sit and burst out crying. One day she got so upset. She went in Armani's room and packed up the crib, changing table, toys, and whatever else she could pack in the van. The kids jumped in the van with her. Tina, Zeek, and Terri (Zeek's friend) got in the van too.

Dana felt so mad, she just wanted to hit something real hard. She ran the van into a fence and started to back up and hit it again, until she heard Tina yell at her real loud. Dana stopped and looked and realized they were with her in the van. She put the van in park, then got out and looked to see the damage that she would have to explain to Chase. Dana was hoping that Tina didn't Tina didn't think her mother lost control. Dana played it off as though it was a mistake. Dana knew she needed some kind of help; she didn't want to feel like she was losing her mind.

Dana went back to her job health department to see the psychiatrist again. This time she drank a large coffee and worked up a smiling face. He wasn't in, but the person who was sent Dana back to work. Dana joined a weight program for someone to help control her eating habits. She joined a gym to work out her anger. Dana tried running a treadmill, whatever to help wear her body down from her mean thoughts. Dana didn't understand why it hurt so much. It was supposed to stop after the funeral. The only thing that stopped was the phone calls from the family and friends. The people she thought would come and drag her out to do things when Chase was away.

When Dana returned to work, a coworker had picked up a collection to have a portrait of Armani made for Dana. Dana was so pleased. She gave her one of her favorite pictures to make the portrait of. Dana cried and thanked her so much.

Chapter

EIGHTEEN

Dana was back at work, and everyone she worked with, she would tell them Armani's story. No one ever told her, but Dana felt people were tired of hearing about this sad story, so she stopped talking about her. Dana started writing her thoughts down on paper about what happened to Armani. She didn't want people to think she was losing her mind, so writing kept her in control.

One day Dana put her notebook on the kitchen table while she was cooking dinner, and all of a sudden, she heard Tina yell, "Oh my god, Mom!"

Dana turned around and said, "What!"

Tina yelled, "You held Armani while she was dead!"

Dana looked at her in amazement; she realized that Tina just read her thoughts without her talking about it. Dana replied, "Yes, I didn't tell you that."

Tina said, "No, Mom, you never told me about that."

Dana thought wow, she can write her thoughts on paper and not even talk about it, but still express her feelings on paper.

Jessica, Dana's coworker, called to tell Dana to pick up the portrait. When Dana picked up the picture, she cried as she looked at it. The portrait looked just like the picture. Jessica had done a wonderful thing for Dana, more than she probably knew. Jessica needed a ride to pick up her car. Dana took her to pick up her car. On the way back, Jessica was following Dana. Dana put a tape in the tape player while she was driving. After one song, the second song that came on was "Only for a While." The song shook Dana up. Dana could hardly see the road. Tears were running down her face. She was in the middle of a three lane-street in the left lane and could not pull over. She tried to pull herself together. She pushed the eject button to stop the tape. Dana hadn't heard that song since Armani was alive.

Dana moved over one lane at a time to the right till it was safe to pull over. Once she was safe in the service lane, she looked in the mirror and saw Jessica was behind her. Dana got out and told Jessica what happened. Jessica told Dana to bring the tape to her car so she can listen to the song with her. As they listened to the song, Dana explained Armani's expression from every word of the song. She smiled even as the tears dropped from her eyes.

Whenever she sang that part to Armani, she remembered wiping the tears from her eye, and Armani would burst out laughing really hard. Jessica said she understood. Sometimes she heard a song that reminded her of something that would make her cry too. She told Dana that she was glad she was there to share that moment with her.

Dana headed home, pulled in the drive, and ran in the house. She took down Chase's picture of a horn and put the picture of Armani up. And there it remained.

Dana continued to write, and then she started to have dreams. One dream was Armani was standing in front of her brushing her hair. It was really long. When she passed away, she had no hair. Dana was sitting in a chair with Zeek in her arms. Zeek had a board head, and he was sick. When Dana woke up from that dream, she told Chase and Zeek. Zeek wanted to ride his bike, and Dana told him he had to wear his helmet. He complained that he didn't want to. Dana told him Armani came to her in that dream to put on his helmet or don't ride his bike. He put on his helmet and went out to ride his bike. A few minutes later, Dana and Chase heard a car crash. They ran to the door. Zeek had jumped off his bike and ran to Dana and Chase. A car crashed into a car right across from the house. Two young boys jumped out and ran.

Chase looked at Dana and said, "Armani was warning you to be careful with Zeek." He looked at Dana in shock.

The next dream Dana had, she was holding Armani while she was deceased, when all of a sudden, her eyes opened, and she started smiling. Dana was happy and smiling. She showed Tina and Zeek. She said, "Look, Armani is alive. Look, she's smiling." Zeek touched her face. Dana told him to be careful.

When Dana woke up from that dream, she told Chase. Chase told Dana that was Armani's way of telling her that she was happy where she was at. After that, Dana slowly started try to let her go. Dana had already written a book about what happened to Armani. She decided to write about something totally different. Dana began to write screenplay after screenplay for years as a hobby. She wrote all different kinds of screenplays, from gospel to action and drama.

Chapter

NINETEEN

Five years later, after Dana got control of her life, she was in the shower doing a breast exam when she noticed a lump on her left breast. Dana decided to ignore it because she had been through that road before. Dana had a lump on her right breast, which was from a past surgery when she was young. It turned out to be scar tissue. She figured why go to the doctor? She felt it was nothing to worry about. She went on with her life as normal.

Tina had grown up, married, and moved out and was pregnant. Dana was excited about becoming a grand-mother. As the days went by, that lump on her breast would not go away. When she touched it, she felt the soreness. Dana began to worry, but was afraid to face it. She finally mentioned it to Pam. Pam insisted that she go to the doctor to get it checked. Dana promised she would, but she never did. Pam was so busy with her three-year-old daughter she had in 2000 that she didn't push Dana to keep her promise.

Dana remembered the day Pam had her daughter. Dana, Chase, and Zeek were driving up to Boston to see the baby, and Dana was doing the driving. Zeek yelled, "By the time we get there, the baby will be walking." Chase thought that was so funny, but Dana was so mad, she didn't want to drive anymore. Somehow and some way, they did make it there before baby Penny was walking.

The pain from the lump in Dana's chest never went away. Dana was watching a TV show one day, a police show. One of the detectives was diagnosed with cancer. He refused to accept it and didn't want treatment. He wouldn't accept any calls from his doctor. The detective and his wife had just had a baby. The doctor got in touch with his wife and told her about her husband's condition. The wife approached him in tears, begging him to get help. That she and the baby both needed him, and they don't want to lose him.

As Dana watched the show, she was in tears, and she couldn't stop crying herself. That scene convinced Dana to pick up the phone and call her doctor and schedule an appointment for the next day.

In the doctor's office, Dana still hadn't told the doctor her real reason for going to see him. Until it was time for him to examine her, then she told him. She said, "The reason I came to see you was for the lump on my breast."

He looked at her and said, "Really? Where?"

Dana showed him, then he did a breast exam. He told Dana that she was a brave woman. He sent her to get a mammogram.

As soon as Dana left, she called to schedule for a mammogram. When she told them she found a lump, they told her to come in right away that day. Then things started moving so fast right after the biopsy. Her doctor was calling her to tell her those words no woman in world ever wants to hear.

She was diagnosed with breast cancer.

All she could do was cry; she thought her life was over. Dana had just become a proud grandmother of a little boy. Dana wanted to be around to see him grow up. Tina planned to stay at the house with the baby to help Dana out after her painful surgery. Dana dreaded what was next to come after the doctor told her that some cancer cells could have escaped into the duct in the breast, and that they removed eight lymph nodes, and three of them were cancerous. She recommended that to make sure all the cancer cells were gone, she would have to do chemotherapy and radiation or remove the whole breast. Dana refused to remove her breast, so she decided to do the treatment.

When Dana met the hematologist, he smiled as he described the chemo treatment. It confused Dana. She didn't know if he was being pleasant or just laughing at her. So she asked him, "Why you are smiling?"

He said he didn't want to tell her this disturbing information with a sad face. He wanted to encourage her to stay happy and stress-free. He told her that sometimes the hair falls out, and some women find that hard to deal with.

Dana thought that she would be one of the women who would not lose her hair. It turned out that after her first treatment, Dana began to feel needles in her head when she was sleeping. She refused to comb her hair because she was afraid it would fall out. No matter what way she lay down, the needle was all over. Dana couldn't sleep. She had to sleep on her face to rest.

It's been two weeks, and she needed to wash her hair, and when she tried, her hair matted up. She couldn't finish washing or combing; all she could do was cut it off. She yelled to Chase to cut it into a short haircut. When he tried, it was spotted with bald spots. So he had to cut her whole head bald.

Dana looked in the mirror and scared herself. She started to cry. Chase held her and told her it would grow back when the treatment was over. He walked her in the room and began to kiss her all over. He made mad passionate love to her, and then they began to laugh at her new hairstyle.

They both went upstairs to introduce Zeek to his mother's new hairstyle. Zeek was shocked, but he understood since Dana did get him prepared for it. Chase and Zeek both cut their heads bald to make Dana feel welcome. It still didn't help. Every time Dana saw herself in the mirror, it frightened her. So she kept a scarf on her head and put on a hat when she went out. She tried to wear a wig, but with no hair, there was nothing to secure it on her head.

Dana and Chase went out to the mall, and she put on her wig. It was so hot, her head would sweat and cause her head to itch. Dana tried to scratch it, and the whole wig moved. Dana was so embarrassed as she tried to straighten the wig out on her head.

After the first session of the chemo, some of Dana's hair began to grow. Dana used vegetable dye to color it so it could show more.

Dana was to begin radiation. She was given cream to put on before she arrived. She had to go every day. The first week, she didn't notice anything. By the second week, her skin in the areas that were radiated began to burn. The burns were so bad, Dana's skin was bleeding under the breast, on her back, and under her arms. The doctor told her to put on more cream. Dana never wanted to go out. It was too painful to wear a bra or even clothes.

Her hair was growing and looking nice, and her breast was bleeding and burned. Dana could not wait until it was all over.

As soon as six weeks of radiation was finished, her second session of chemo started. And what little hair that grew on her head fell out again.

Dana tried to do things to help keep her spirits up. She always told Zeek that he played video games so much that she was going to write a song about him. One day she sat in her backyard and wrote that song in fifteen minutes. Then she ran upstairs to sing it on her tape recorder so she would not forget the melody. As she was recording the song, she looked out the window and saw Zeek walking home from school. Dana could not wait to approach Zeek with the song.

As soon as he came in the house, she told him she wrote him the song, and did he want to hear it? Zeek just looked at her. Dana was so excited about it, she started to sing it to him. Once she finished, she ask him if he liked it. Zeek said, "It's alright" and walked out.

Dana was a little hurt. She walked downstairs to the basement with Chase and told him that she wrote a cute little song for Zeek, but he acted like he didn't even care about it. Chase said, "Really? Sing it for me, let me hear it."

As Dana sang the song, Chase had a little smile on his face. Once she finished, he told her, "You know, you got a little talent there."

Dana was shocked that he liked it. He encouraged her to make the song.

Dana taught Zeek and his friend the song and took them to the studio. Zeek didn't have as much passion for singing as his friend, so he let him split the lead parts of the song. Then she invested in video that she had shot at the house, and she used the neighborhood kids. The video got lost by an editor, and Dana never saw it again. Later she shot another video, and this time she had the video and the CD to the song. Dana started taking them to sing at a few children's birthday parties and adoption agency parties for foster children. Zeek decided he didn't want to do it anymore. Dana respected his wishes. Then she started back writing to help keep her from the depression moments.

Chemo was destroying all the good cells as well as the bad in Dana. She would always get a nasty taste in her mouth. She would always eat something to take it away, but it always came back. Dana gained a lot of weight. Her bones in her whole body was always hurting. Every time she went from chemo, her blood count was low. The doctor always had to give her a shot to bring it back up. The chemo was breaking Dana down. Sometimes she would go in the bathroom and quietly cry and pray that she live through this, and sometimes she felt like she wasn't going to make it. She tried to stay away from negative people.

Chase used to drag her out of the house to help keep her mind clear, to shop, walk, movies, anything to keep her from sitting at home wallowing in sad feelings. He took her to a fish market one day right after she had chemo. Dana got so sick from the smell, she couldn't eat the whole day. Dana began to cook with lots of garlic, onions, and peppers to help her fight off her nausea feeling from the chemo.

Chase built a studio in the basement for Dana to learn how to make music for some of the songs she wrote or to continue writing her screenplays. And that is exactly what she did. Once all Dana's treatment was finished, Dana returned to work. She wrote during midnight, on her lunch break, on anything she could find. Toilet paper or any available paper at the time she could grab when a thought came in her mind. Then she would go home in the morning and sleep, and when she woke up, she grabbed her scrap papers and put them on the computer for her screenplay.

Once she finished writing it, she would print it out and take it to work for one of her best readers to read. Once they read it, they would give her their feedback. Then she would hand it to the next critical reader. She would get their likes or dislikes and make corrections on the screenplay as she felt needed until she was happy with her work. Then she moved on to her next project.

Chapter

TWENTY

Dana was driving from the gym one afternoon. While waiting for the light to change to make a left turn, the left-turning signal came on, and she proceeded to make her turn. A van passed the stoplight and drove in and tail-ended Dana's van. Her car spun around in the middle of the street. Dana was in a daze before she realized where she was. Traffic was coming it seemed like in all directions. She turned back on the car and pulled it over to a side to feel safe. Her whole left side was in pain where she had her surgery.

Chase met her there at the scene while the police was filling out the accident report. Dana went to the hospital after the accident and for physical therapy. She would have never known that it could have been the cause of her to develop lymphedema. Some months later, that is exactly what happened. Dana's arm slowly began to swell that she didn't really notice it was happening. Dana began to worry about her work condition with her arm in constant pain. She knew that if a fight broke out, she wouldn't be much help. She didn't want to go on medical monitor because there was no cure for lymphedema. The department would eventually medically separate her, so she retired as soon as she could.

Her first day of retirement was her first day in her new life. Dana called her mother and told her to pack her bags and clear her calendar for the week. She picked up her mother and headed for a road trip, just her and her mother. Dana took her mother to visit every one of her children who moved away from New York. Acee first. They stayed the first night with her in Virginia. Acee cooked a big dinner and invited their brother Rob and his wife and kids and his grandchild. Acee's older son, his wife, and son came over too. Adele enjoyed seeing everyone. It was her first time meeting her grandson's wife and her great-grandson and daughter. She didn't think she was going be able to visit them after here surgery with colon cancer. They were all glad to see her in their part of town. They all laughed and had a good time.

The next morning they set out to pull out at five in the morning. Acee's husband had already made them a nice big breakfast before they left.

The next stop was North Carolina to visit Cindy, which was a two-hour drive. Dana and her mother talked about back in the days all the way. They talked and joked about when Dana and her siblings were growing up. The fights they had, parties, family get-togethers. Dana was totally excited hearing about her mother growing up in the south. She got so into it, she didn't realize how fast she was driving. There were two big tractor trailers. Dana drove past them. Before she could slow down, she saw the patrol car on the side that pulled out right behind Dana.

As she pulled over, she asked her mother if they were going to give her a ticket. Her mother said, "Yes, they pulled you over." Dana had no way of talking herself out of that ticket. She didn't even honor her shield. Dana sped off angrily with a ticket in her hand. Dana told her mother it was her fault for having such good conversation with her. Her mother laughed and said, "You going to blame me? You were talking too."

All Dana could do was laugh and say, "I can't believe I was driving 83 on a 65 speed limit."

The rest of the way, Adele would read the speed limit to Dana to keep her mind on track. They finally reached Cindy's house for a quick break. They stayed a couple of hours before heading farther out in North Carolina another three hours. Dana drove Adele to visit her brother and nieces and nephew. Dana stayed one night there and left Adele there to spend time with her brother. Dana when back to Cindy's house to spend three days with her.

After her visit with Cindy, she went back to stay with Adele. The next day, Dana loaded up Adele, two of her nieces, and her brother and took a two-hour drive to South Carolina to Dana's older brother, Claude. They spent the day with him and then drove back to North Carolina for the last night of the trip.

On the trip home, they stopped back at Cindy's house to pick up her husband, who was taking a trip back to New York to help Dana on the drive back. He drove back four hours, and Dana drove the last four hours that ended the road trip.

Dana enjoyed being retired for a whole year before she decided to go back to work for retail.

Chapter

TWENTY-ONE

Dana went back to working overnight. While she was working, she was working trying to produce one of her screenplays. An old friend of hers came up with a nice proposal that her and him along with another director get together and work it so each of them can shoot one of each of their movies. Of course, his movie had to be shot first.

They all set out to find investors. Dana went straight to the strongest person she knew who had the money to invest. They set up the meeting. He loved the idea and was ready to invest. They were about to shoot their first movie. Until the day they had the meeting that killed the whole project. This meeting, the investor got to meet the third party. Once he found out that he had all the equipment and the amount of the percentage he was getting almost was more than what he was getting, he backed out of the project. Dana's old friend was so hurt and lost after running around looking for a location and actors that he promised parts in the movie.

Dana ventured out to do a simple low-budget film. She found another investor who told her to give him the budget. When she did, he asked her to make it lower. The budget was revised to a lower budget. He asked her to make it lower, and Dana thought it was too low that she found it as an insult.

Dana decided that she would invest in her own movie. When she told her friend her plan, he was more than happy to join her in producing the movie. The director was on board too; he said he would supply the cameras. Dana found all the locations. They set up an account for casting and the dates and location. Dana would work all night and was up all day checking all the e-mails that were coming in from actors for the part. It was about 250 a day. It was the hardest job in the world, she thought, but her blood was racing. It kept her going constantly.

She was too busy to feel the pain from her lymphedema in her arm that she didn't realize it was getting bigger. This was the best thing for her; it was like her passion. Time was getting closer; it was time to find the crew and rent the equipment. Before she knew it, she was picking up a truck and all of this equipment; she was setting up the house for the first shoot.

Early the next morning, Dana had the caterer stop by to do the cooking. She was driving all over, picking up actors and crew members from the train station. Dana's heart was racing because this was about to happen. Dana was in her house set up as the holding. In the basement and the upstairs were where the first shots were going to take place. Her two partners were stuck in the city still trying to get the right insurance to get some equipment for the camera, which took part of the day. The first shot was about six hours late. Thank god for Dana that the crew and actors were very patient with food and games to help keep them keep kind of calm.

The moment they started to shoot, Dana had to run to the bathroom to compose herself from the tears filling in her eyes. She could not believe all these actors and crew member that she never even met until the audition. That they were here in her house to be a part of the movie she wrote. Dana tried to get herself together and dry her eyes. She could hear the director/photographer yell, "Where is Dana? We need Dana here before I can shoot!"

That's when Dana wiped away her last tear and walked out the door and went on the set as the first director. It was the most beautiful thing she ever witnessed, watching the actors give it their all to portray their character. Looking at the monitor, it was amazing.

Tina came by the house with Dana's grandson. He walked around confused of what was going on in his Nana's house. Dana walked him around and introduced him to the actors and explained some of the equipment. He got so curious, he started touching things, so Tina rushed him out of the house.

Dana was being called to help find clothing for wardrobe and make sure the actors in makeup were ready for their shot. She had to make sure the food was prepared on time. Dana could not stay on the set and just direct. She had to relinquish that position of the director to the second director and have him direct. She second directed. That gave her more flexibility to move around.

After instructing her actors on what she wanted from them and a couple of quick rehearsals, the other director did his thing. Dana was in and out checking the shots, making sure there were a few good ones in for the editor to work with.

Dana was sick with a bad cough that she couldn't get rid of. She took cough medication and some Halls candy and drank plenty of hot tea. Some of the cast members were even trying to help to make sure they could finish shooting the movie. One actor brought in a special remedy for Dana to take to help stop her cough, which made her feel a lot better.

Chase helped a lot. He set up the family room to look like an office. He took the art designer to pick up props. He also drove the caterer to pick up food supplies. He dropped by the sets to check to see if Dana needed his help, which she did. She needed him to become an actor for a no-show. He quickly jumped into action and started studying the role. It turned out that he played two different parts that day. He brought Zeek and two of his friends, and they all took part in the movie. Zeek's little friend Steven played a major role after Dana finished working with him. She put in the role after putting him in the mindset that this was happening in his real life. Steven's whole expression changed, and he became the character Dana was looking for.

They shot the whole movie in ten days with one day off. A few days after the movie was completed, Dana received a delivery of a beautiful fruit bouquet with a note from Tina, saying, "Congratulations, Mommy, on your success on the making of your movie." Dana was so surprised and happy that Tina, her daughter, was proud of her.

The completed unedited movie sat in the procession of the first director's editing studio for about a year. Dana got impatient and told him to give the hard drives to her, and she will get the movie completed. That was exactly what Dana did. She traveled to Jersey or Brooklyn with the hard drive. Spent countless hours waiting for the work to be done, not leaving all her hard work and invested money spent in the hands of no one. She would take the hard drives for the audio and editing the day they had time to work on it. Giving them all of her imprint on what she wanted. Dana put together all the music for the soundtrack. She put together every sound that she needed for each part and sound effect. She took her small microphone out to pick up live sounds.

Sometimes she didn't get home till late at night or early in the morning, until she got a product that she could send out to get the movie picked up. Dana felt like she owed her actors and cast that much to help them grow from the production. Dana never gave up.

Finally, she received a call from the president of Maverick Entertainment, a distributor company, that he was interested in the movie.

Dana could not believe that all her hard work paid off well, not in money, but just one foot in the door for all that took part in the project. The actors signed a contract that was done by the producer. She didn't trust this, and she put the movie under another company and had to get the contracts signed over again. Dana was back at work again, finding all the actors and crew members to sign contacts again.

Dana hadn't started her own company yet and was so anxious to get the movie out for the actors and crew that she didn't care that she was losing money. Dana had to send the hard drives to the distributor but refused to send it through postal service. She trusted no one. So she set up to take it to them herself. She had to go to Charlotte to spend a week with Pam to take care of her. Pam had just got over pneumonia, and being that she only had one lung, they had to put her on a respirator so her lung could heal. The cousins set up to share the time to go and help take care of her and her daughter.

After Dana's week there, Pam was feeling great. So Dana took the hard drives that she traveled with to Charlotte to Orlando, Florida. Dana met up with her friend Roberta. The next day, they drove five hours to meet and delivered the hard drives to the movie. This turned out to be a long journey because Dana never produced a movie. She was still learning, and now she was working with Maverick Entertainment, who mounted her on their horse and helped her all the way.

It was almost time for the movie to come out, and Dana's mother was so proud of her. Adele used to have to yell at Dana and tell her that she needed to get some rest. Dana and her older sister would go to visit her mother once a week to do her hair or shopping or cleaning. After Dana finished, she would curl up on the couch and fall asleep, while her older sister cooked her mother's dinner. Dana's mother was still being treated for cancer, so Dana and her sisters all had different days to go over and take care of her. Even though she had an aide, they all tried to be there for her as much as possible.

The movie had a release date to come out. Dana had a telephone interview to with a reporter to talk about her inspiration on what made her write and produce the movie. She received the phone call when she was bringing her mother back from the doctor's office. Dana was driving her mother to pick up her prescription and had to apologize for some interruption. So she pulled over to the side to complete the interview. One of the actors from the movie scheduled a radio interview with Dana and told her to bring five other actors to talk about the movie. Dana told the distributing company about the radio interview, and they began to advertise it. Dana told her mother Adele about the radio interview that was coming up. She made Dana set her radio to the station right then and there, so when the day came, she could just turn it on and listen to it.

Dana and her older sister took Adele for a doctor's appointment. The doctor explained to them that the chemo pills Adele was taking wasn't doing anything for her and that the cancer has continued to spread. The doctor asked Dana if she wanted the doctor or nurse to start to come and see Adele in her house. Dana turned and looked at Adele, and to her, Adele looked strong and was moving fine. Dana said no, she didn't want to lock and confine her mother to the house.

Back at Adele's house, she had Dana and Trudy go through paperwork and told them there were important things there and for them to look through all of them and throw out what she didn't need.

A couple of days later, Adele stopped eating. Cindy had come up for Thanksgiving. On Thanksgiving eve, while they all were there, Adele was not acting normal. They tried to get her to eat or drink something, but she didn't seem to respond. Dana went behind Adele and whispered in her ear, "Lady, you better eat your food." Adele only smiled.

When they left, they asked a niece to come over and spend some time with Adele. They were all concerned of her weird behavior. Cindy returned home after the holiday. One Monday morning, Tina took off from work to go spend the day with Adele. When she got there, the ambulance was taking Adele out of the building. Tina called Dana and told her what was going on. Dana thought Tina said she had a dream. She didn't understand what made Tina take the day off work. Once Dana understood what she was saying, she immediately picked up Trudy and raced to the hospital.

Trudy was on the phone with Clare, so Dana ran into the emergency room and asked for Adele. One nurse directed her to bed number 4. When Dana got there, they were digging and poking in Adele's private area, trying to get urine or place a tube in her. Adele was screaming in pain. Dana grabbed her head, wanting to yell at them to stop, and at the same time she wanted them to help her mother. So she stood outside the curtain and put her hands together and prayed until they finished. Adele was calm, her eyes rolling from side to side. Dana called her mom, "Can you hear me?"

Adele looked at her with her mouth opening and closing, and her chin was shaking. Dana grabbed her hand. She looked at her again and stopped shaking. She just looked straight up toward the ceiling. Trudy walked in the room and asked Dana what they said. She told her nothing yet.

Right then, a female doctor walked in. She asked Dana and Trudy to step out so she can talk to them.

She said that the cancer had incapacitated Adele's whole liver. Dana was shocked listening to the doctor tell Trudy that the cancer had spread all over and if they wanted to resuscitate her if anything happened. Trudy said, "Yes, do what you can for her." Dana stood quietly thinking.

Once they were outside the room, Dana told Trudy that she thinks they should all decide if they want to resuscitate. Because once they put her on it, it will be hard to get her off. Trudy agreed, and they started to make phone calls to the other siblings. They all knew Adele didn't want to be on a machine. As hard as it was for them all, they all agreed to let her go peacefully.

Dana told Trudy when she walked in the room, they had Adele screaming and that she could not take hearing her mother in pain like that. Trudy admitted that she thought everyone would get mad at her if she didn't have them do all they can to keep Adele alive. Dana told her they would, but right now, there was nothing they can do if the cancer was taking over.

Carol came to the hospital alone. She said Loren couldn't make it as she was with her husband who just got out of jail. Trudy said Adele said she's never going to see her again. Dana yelled, "No, Carol! You have to make her come. Mom needs to see her before she is gone." Carol promised she will try to get her there. Adele was moved to ICU.

The next day when Dana and Trudy got to her room, Carol called and said they were downstairs, and they wouldn't let them up. Trudy went to the desk and told them what was going on. The nurse at the desk called down and gave clearance to let them upstairs.

When they came up in the room, it was Carol, Loren, and Adele's best friend. She was so upset because she had to leave to go on her trip to visit family. The sisters convinced her to go on with her plans. She's been nothing but more than a friend to their mother. Nothing is going to change if she canceled her trip. They promised to keep in touch with her about what was going on. She cried and said her goodbyes to her old friend and had to leave for her trip. They all knew this day would come.

Loren went to Adele's side and said to her, "Mom, it's me, Loren."

Adele opened her eyes and looked at her and yelled, "God help me! Lord have mercy!"

They all looked in shock and then looked at each other. Adele had not spoken a word since she was in the hospital.

Loren said, "Mom, yes, I'm here."

They all tried to understand what just happened. Before they could figure it out, they were interrupted by a doctor who came in to speak to them. He escorted them into a bigger room. He told them that her kidneys were breaking down and that they would have to put a needle in her neck to do dialysis.

Dana told them, "No please, just leave her alone. What is that going to do, buy them more time to experiment on her?"

159

He explained that they had to move the wires to the other side to keep her from infection. Trudy and Carol told Dana to let them do that, and Dana agreed to that only.

The doctor sent in a young lady to speak to them and explain about what was hospice. She took them on a tour to make them feel comfortable about it.

When they returned back to Adele, another doctor spoke to Dana and Trudy and told them that Adele had about two days to live. Finally it hit home that they were about to lose their mother, the rock of the family. They rushed to make calls to try to get the other siblings home in time to see her before she passed. Trudy signed the papers to put Adele in hospice. The medical staff sent the sisters to go get lunch while they prepared to move Adele to hospice.

The sisters went to the room in hospice. Adele lay there so peacefully. Dana was upset that she still had a tube in her mouth. The nurse came in and started adjusting her bed. Dana asked why was the tube still in her mother's mouth.

The nurse said she didn't know why they didn't remove it. She asked, "Would you like me to take it out?"

Dana said, "Yes, please."

The nurse put on some gloves and removed it gently. Dana thanked her and walked over to her mother and asked Trudy for the little Bible. She opened Adele's hand and placed the Bible in it. Adele held tightly to it. Loren and Carol had to leave, but Dana and Trudy tried to stay as long as they could. They left around nine that night. Dana told Trudy that it was time for them to make arrangements.

Dana dropped Trudy home, and by the time Dana got in the house, Trudy called and told her that their mother had passed. Acee and Cindy and Rob and Claude were on their way home. None of the other siblings traveling made it on time. They were all upset.

Flowers came to Dana's house from Maverick Entertainment, the movie distributing company. They also sent a beautiful card to her and the family. They promised to do a good job with the movie to make Dana's mother proud of her.

Chapter

TWENTY-TWO

The family being together worked together in planning Adele's funeral. They started talking about the past when they were growing up. Dana had her radio interview to do the day before the funeral, which she wanted to cancel, but the family talked her into it for her mother. Dana cried all day trying to get her mind set for the radio interview.

Dana sat in the living room quietly, unable to move. The door opened, and her sister-in-law Brenda walked in. Dana started to cry even harder while sitting in her chair. She knew her mother would have been so happy to see her walking. Some years back, Brenda's daughter died giving birth to her baby girl. Not too long after, Brenda's only remaining son, his wife, and a few other children were in a very bad car accident on the highway to Philadelphia. Brenda's son's head was decapitated. His wife died, and a friend's small baby. Brenda's back was broken. The others had minor injuries.

Dana knew that Adele was really hurt by the loss of her two grandchildren from her son who had passed away many years ago. She felt so bad for Brenda and seeing her in a wheelchair at her son's funeral with a broken back. Dana felt the joy her mother would have felt if she had seen her walking strong after what she'd been through.

Dana got up and hugged her as hard as she could, as if she was hugging her own mother. Seeing her holding up strong after what she'd been through gave Dana the strength to go do the radio interview.

Dana went into her mother's closet and took out one of her scarves and put it on her neck. The family all wished her luck, and Dana and Chase left for the interview.

On the way, Dana tried to prepare herself so she would not break down during the interview. While back at the house, the family struggled to hear the interview over one of their drunken cousins. He refused to stop talking. Zeek, Acee, Trudy, and Carol were all curled up around the radio. They listened to all the other actors and to the soundtrack of songs that Dana introduced.

During the break when the songs were played, all the kids would get up and dance. Dana said in the interview that the movie was to help encourage young hip-hop singers change their way of rapping by turning the N-word into something nice, the B-word to beautiful, and F-word to fabulous and become a little more creative for the younger generation. She never mentioned that her mother had passed away because she knew she would not be able to continue the interview. She did tell the other actors so that they would do most of the talking to help her out.

Dana was so glad when everything was over, the radio interview and the funeral. Cleaning up Adele's apartment was the hardest thing she ever had to do. Christmas came and went, and none of the family got together to do anything like they would have if Adele was alive. Acee called crying to say how much she missed her. Cindy, Acee, and Dana would be on the phone trying to make it through the holidays, but with each of them in different states, it didn't make it easy for them.

Dana returned to her part-time job. While Dana was working, she received an email from the distributor company that the release day for the DVD was set for January 10, and that it can be preordered. Dana informed all the actors and their family and friends about that information. Dana posted it online and had her family and friends and their friends and family spread the word. Dana made up little cards with the movie cover and the link to view the trailer and where to go to order the DVD. The actors and cast and crew were so excited that the move made it on DVD. Dana was praying that it would open doors for all of them; she didn't really care about the investment she loss. She felt that with all their hard work and dedication to her, she owed them that much. So she never gave up on pushing the movie.

The day the DVD *Book of Songs* was released, Chase went and picked a copy up from Blockbuster's new releases. He brought it to Dana's job. Dana was so excited, she left her post and took it around to show the principal, the assistant principal, and her coworkers. Most of them had already ordered and were waiting for their copy to come in.

By the time Dana got home from work, most of the actors were calling Dana, excited their copy came in. They thanked Dana for including them in the project.

The next day, Dana received her fifteen copies in the mail. She quickly delivered the copies to the family. Chase's family and friends in Boston were so excited about the roles that Chase played in the movie. Cindy and some of her friends placed an order as well. Cindy bragged about her sister to all her husband's family and what few friends she had. In time, she found out that her friends were the most supportive of her sister's success.

The distributing company called Dana with some good news that the movie was going to be sold in a major stores for about a week for promotion. Dana of course let all of her family and friends, the actors, and crew members know when and where to buy it. Dana and Chase went to the store and signed autographs, and they sold out that day. Cindy had all the people she knew who worked in the store she worked in know that her sister wrote and produced the movie, and her store sold out.

Most of the workers in Cindy's store were so impressed. Cindy had two good friends who looked out for her when she moved to North Carolina. Cindy moved there with no friends and only family from her husband's side. She was very unhappy. Cindy's friends Myron and Lisa had never met Dana but were truly inspired by her. They wanted to do something for her to show their love support of North Carolina. They planned to have an honorary banquet for Dana and some of the main actors. Myron was in charge of it all since it was she who planned to do it. She felt that the movie changed her life. She wanted Cindy to help her make it a surprise for Dana, but Cindy had no way of contacting the actors. She told Myron that she had to let Dana know what she was planning. Myron called Dana and asked if she could give a banquet in honor of her and the cast, and would she and Chase and Zeek and some of the main characters attend. Dana was surprised and said yes, she and her family would, but she had to check with the actors.

Dana got six of the actors to accept the invitation. Myron sent out tickets for Dana to sell to family and friends who were willing to travel for the event. Myron was promoting the event in North Carolina. She had set up a newspaper interview and a radio interview for Dana to come out herself in person to help promote the event. Dana and the actors were very excited about the event.

Myron decided to pick Dana up from New York, and she and a friend would escort her to North Carolina. Kerry was in New York, so she rode back with them. On the ride, Dana got to know this person who went out of her way to promote her movie. Dana already knew that she was a lesbian, but she got to know her more as a person.

Myron showed Dana wedding pictures when she was married to a man. Dana was shocked. Myron told her she was in love with a woman at the time. Dana yelled at her and told her, "Why you would marry a man when you know you wanted to be with a woman?" Dana did not think it was fair for Myron to do that to the man that she married.

Myron said that she knew he and her sister were trying to change her lifestyle, but it didn't work. Dana was mad. It reminded her of those down-low men who married and had kids with a woman just to keep their secret. How can they put someone in the middle of their true lifestyle is the worst thing to do.

Dana told her about a friend who found a video of her husband having sex with a man. She was so upset that she took their son to a hotel and shot him, then called the police and told them she shot her son, and then she shot herself. Myron told Dana she knew and that she was trying to be who she wanted to be. That it was so hard for her that she ended up having a heart attack. So that's why she fights so hard for equality for all.

Myron had a very busy week set up for Dana. The next day, Myron picked Dana up to take her for a newspaper interview. A white gray-headed older man stood outside waiting for them. He put his hand out to shake Myron's hands. "Myron, it's good to see you."

She introduced Dana. The man shook her hand and congratulated her on her DVD, *Book of Songs*. He thought it was a great inspirational movie. He escorted them inside. There was newspaper all over the place. They entered a back room where one gentleman was typing. He started to question her and take pictures. They joked and had fun, and sometimes it got real serious when he hit home base with questions about Armani or Dana's cancer. It was very difficult for Dana to explain how she came to write or produce the movie. She answered the question sharp and quick to get past thinking about it too much.

He told them that the article would be in the paper the next day.

Dana then started getting calls from Myron and Cindy's in-laws that she was on the first page. The next day, Myron took Dana for a radio interview. Dana was afraid to talk on the radio, even though she did it before, but with five other guests, and that made it easy for her. This one she will be alone.

When they got to the radio station, the young lady who was supposed to do the interview called in sick. Myron was so upset, so she decided to do the interview herself. She told Dana, "Don't worry, I got you. I'm going to interview you. This is what we're going to do. Pick out the songs you want to play from the *Book of Songs* soundtrack."

Dana wrote down the songs in order and gave it to the DJ. Myron and Dana went in to the booth. Myron started the segment with a prayer and then introduced the writer, director, and executive producer of the DVD movie *Book of Songs*.

Dana said, "Hello, North Carolina! I'm so glad to be here."

Myron talked about the banquet that was taking place and where to purchase tickets. She asked questions about the movie and what inspired Dana to write and produce it.

Cindy and Kerry sat outside in the car listening to the segment. Once the interview was over, Dana threw herself back in the chair and exhaled. Myron just laughed at her and told her not to worry, it's over. Dana asked Myron who was that person who just interviewed her. Dana was shocked Myron started out with a prayer and quoted verses from the Bible like a preacher.

Myron told Dana that she was a pastor and that she had to leave the church because of her style of life. Cindy and Kerry both agreed that Myron spoke so well and that she did a great interview with Dana.

The next day was set up to be a telephone interview with a much bigger radio station. They told Dana she can come in or do the interview on the radio. Dana decided to do it by telephone so she can be a little more confident. Myron and Cindy wanted Dana to try not to say "and um," getting stuck on her words.

The radio host called Dana to discuss the interview. He asked her what her story was. As Dana told him, he thought it was very interesting to hear. So he set up the time for Dana to be at a landline for the interview. Once Dana had a secure landline, she waited patiently for the scheduled time to call in.

Pam was on the road to come to Cindy's house, so she was set up to listen in the car on the road. A few old friends from Dana's old job who lived about an hour away set up to listen as well.

Dana called in the radio station, and it was a live taping. Dana was in the room alone, and she spoke strongly and confidently as she answered the questions and gave advice to any young or older person to stop mourning and start growing. Dana gave out her website where people can view the trailer and her phone number if they wanted more information about her next project.

Once Dana completed the interview and walked out the room, everybody was so happy. It was a great interview. Dana just exhaled. She didn't think she could make it through that week speaking to a newspaper reporter on the radio about her personal life. It was time to relax and celebrate.

Once Pam arrived, they went out for dinner and drinks.

Dana went walking with Cindy, Myron, and Lisa on the track. It was something they did faithfully every morning. Lisa told Dana that she should write a movie about her life, that she could make a lot of money after all that she's been through. Dana laughed and said, "Really? Tell me, Lisa, what's your story?"

She told them that when she was thirteen years old, she was raped by three men who left her for dead. They buried her under bricks and dirt and tree limbs. They didn't find her until three days later. How her husband beat her for years. She was scared to leave him. She caught him cheating on her, and he beat her from going out of the house. He made her sleep in the bathtub filled with ice water all night, and when she tried to get out, he would knock her back in it. She talked about three women trying to rape her. Lisa went on about a boyfriend who kicked her so hard in her stomach while she was pregnant that she lost the baby.

They got so into her stories that they walked about seven miles instead of five.

Dana said, "Oh my god, that's a book by itself."

Lisa has been through so much. She knew without the grace of God, she wouldn't be alive. They were all shook up by her story and though that she should have had some professional help.

Dana's mind started to imagine Lisa's life on screen. Dana asked her if she would be able to tell the world about her life. Lisa said she was not ashamed of her life; she was happy to be alive.

They all agreed and jumped in the car to go to breakfast after a good walk.

Chapter

TWENTY-THREE

Dana was back in New York when she decided to work on a new screenplay to help keep her mind off all her debt that she made while making the movie *Book of Songs*. Dana never regretted the things she did to produce her movie. It was what she needed to help fight away her pain and negative thoughts in her life.

Chase, Zeek, and even Tina all respected her whenever she was writing. They all left her alone. If she got too involved in what she was writing and forgot about dinner, Chase would run out and pick up something for dinner so Dana could continue her writing. Dana wanted to challenge herself. She was writing two screenplays at one time: a children's screenplay and a drama. One day she would work on one and the next day the other.

She finished the drama, and the children's screenplay she got halfway done. She thought it would be best to work on one screenplay and get it completely completed, then move to the next.

Dana wrote and at the same time spent all of her time trying to promote the DVD movie that was out. Everywhere she went and everyone she met, she told them about her movie. On her doctor's appointment, Dana would discuss how happy she was to be alive. They knew about every project that Dana was working on through each visit. Some of them even purchased the movie. The doctor who did Dana's breast surgery bragged about Dana to her secretary. She said, "I was watching a movie, and I saw someone I knew."

Dana laughed and told her, "I forgot to tell you that I was in my own movie."

One of the secretaries was so excited, she asked Dana, "Did you actually write the movie?"

Dana told her, "I did more than that. I wrote, executive produced, and directed it. If I took any more credit, my name would be all over casting, location, and so much more."

They were so impressed that they almost forgot to get her copayment. Dana left and was on her way to the elevator when one of the secretaries ran after Dana to tell her that her daughter went to school for director photographer. Dana took her information if she could ever use her.

Dana got on the elevator in good spirits, wishing that one day she could help a lot of people fulfill their dreams. So many actors, singers, and other experienced people who had so many dreams who were very talented will never get that one big break to take them where they want to be. Dana wished she was in the position to be the one to help them fulfill their dreams.

Ever since Dana got a distributing company to pick up her movie, she gained big respect from the actors and crew involved, and she so much wanted to keep that. Dana had so many people approach her trying to advertise what it was they did professionally. Dana had to let them know that she was still trying to get her foot in the door so she can reach back to help others, and that now she was just writing and praying that God will bless her ability. She would just take their information and give them her information and keep in touch if something came through that they can work together on.

Chapter

TWENTY-FOUR

The actors and Dana's family planned their trip to North Carolina for the banquet. They all had to pay their own travel expenses. Myron already had the rooms set up in the hotel. They would have a meet and greet on Friday, and the banquet would be on Saturday. Six of the main actors had made arrangements to go to the banquet. Dana planned to leave on Thursday night with Chase and Zeek, and three of the actors were going to ride down with them. Two were flying down, and one lived an hour away and was going to drive there the day of the banquet. Tina and her husband and son were going to drive down Friday. Other family and friends were either flying or driving down.

On Thursday while Dana was at work, she started to lose her voice. By the time she got home, she started to drink tea, get some rest, and wait for the other three actors to show up at her house. By the time they arrived, Dana had no voice at all. Dana started out driving because

Chase got off work that morning, and she wanted him be well rested for the overnight drive. On the drive down, Dana could not talk at all. She got so tired of trying to say something, and no one could hear her, so she stopped talking altogether.

It turned out Chase couldn't sleep anyway; in fact, no one could sleep. One of the actors was snoring so loud, it drowned out the radio. Dana drove till two in the morning, then she pulled over to let Chase take over.

They arrived at Cindy's house at six in the morning. Cindy was at the front door to welcome them all to her house. Cindy was surprised Dana lost her voice. She yelled, "You need to stop talking!"

Dana started to cook breakfast, and she asked Cindy for the grits and some tea because coffee wouldn't help her voice. She didn't have any, so she decided to go get some, and she asked Zeek to ride with her. Two of the male actors jumped up and said, "I will ride too."

Cindy looked at Dana as if she was asking should she let them go. Dana said it was okay if it was okay with her. Cindy's husband was very jealous. He would blame Cindy for messing with a man standing in a line behind her.

When they returned with the grits and tea, Dana cooked a nice big breakfast buffet. After a nice big breakfast, they loaded up in the van and met Myron at the hotel to check in. Dana got in the room, took a shower, and got in the bed. Chase and Zeek went out to get Dana some hot tea. Chase and Zeek ran into Acee and Loren when they arrived. Then Pam and Penny arrived. And then two of Dana's friends from her old job arrived, Tonya and Penny. One of the actors had two of their guests arrive.

Later, Dana rode with Myron to pick up one of the actors from the airport. They stopped at a restaurant to get the actress something eat on the way back. Dana was feeling too bad to eat, so she packed hers to go. Everyone made her go to her room and lie back in bed until the meet and greet began. She was ordered not to talk for the rest of the day.

The meet and greet was down the block from the hotel in a Chinese restaurant. Everyone took a slow walk there. The tables were set up in the back with a professional photographer. It was a buffet that was all taken care of by Myron. All the actors were present, including Chase and Zeek, as they were part of the cast. They all sat at one table while everyone came in to meet them and take a picture with them. Then they all would go get a plate of food and have a seat and socialize with the actors.

Dana had strict orders not to talk. If a guest came to speak to Dana, Myron, Lisa, or one of her sisters would tell them that Dana was not allowed to talk. They told her that she had to rest her voice. They all wanted to make sure Dana would be able to say a speech at the banquet.

Everybody retired back to the rooms. Dana went into Carol's and Acee's room with Cindy and Pam. They were drinking, having a good time, hanging out. Acee and Pam decided to fix Dana a drink to get her voice back, some hot tea and rum. Dana so badly wanted to get her voice back, she drank two cups. Then she went back to her room and fell asleep while Zeek and Pam's daughter played video games in the room.

Chase went over to Acee's room to hang out with them. Pam offered them some hot seeds that had Acee crying. Carol pulled out a deck of cards, and they started playing spades. They were drinking and having a good time. Carol took off her wig and had it lying on the table. Acee picked it up and put it on her head, and they all started laughing. Pam took it off her head and put it on her head. Carol got mad and took it and tried to put it back on her head.

Myron went to pick up another actor and his fiancée from the airport. Their plane came in late that night. They even missed the meet and greet. A few of the actors got in the van with Myron and rode with her to pick up another actor and his fiancée.

The next morning, everyone was stopping by Dana's room to see if she was feeling better. She had a voice back a little, but they still wanted her not to talk until the night. Acee came in with some bagels and little muffins and a cup of hot tea for Dana. Chase complained that he wanted a real breakfast. Acee agreed, and they decided to pick up breakfast. Zeek went with them. Dana stayed in the bed and continued to sleep. Chase and Acee came back to the room separating the food, arguing that she had his and that one was Carol's food. Their loud voices woke Dana up. Once they got their food problem sorted out, she went back to her room. Dana ate her food in bed, then got up and took a shower. Everyone seemed to find something to do. Some went to the movies while others shopped. Dana went with Pam to help her find a pair of shoes for the banquet.

In the meanwhile, Myron, Lisa, and Cindy were setting up for the banquet. Before you knew it, it was time to get ready. Myron wanted all the actors to be ready at six downstairs and waiting. Everyone was on time, but she wasn't there yet. One actor noticed that the sign posted outside the hotel said "Welcome to the Book of Songs Cast." Everyone was so excited. The cast went outside to take pictures under it. It was so cold out, but they took off their jackets to pose. The sign was so high up, it was hard trying to get the actors and the sign in one shot. One of the actors had a professional camera that got some really good pictures.

Finally Myron arrived, and they all got in their cars. Chase, Zeek, Dana, and the other actors got in the van. The drive to the banquet was like a mystery. Myron said she wanted them all to stay in the van until she told them to come out. She parked and went inside, then she came out with the other actor who drove straight to the banquet. They all laughed at him and asked him if he got kicked out. They tried to question him to find out what was going on. He didn't know anything; he said he just got there.

Before he could start talking, Myron came out and asked for him. They all looked at each other, trying to figure out what was going on.

Myron came out got one actor at a time and walked them into the banquet. Dana and one other actor were left. When Myron took the last actor, Dana's heart began to race. She was beginning to get scared. Dana had no idea what was planned for her. It all began to fall on her now, that Myron escorted each actor based on their main role in the movie. Why was she the last to go in? Because she was the writer, executive producer, and director?

She began to get nervous and questioned herself if she could handle the fame. She watched Myron walk out and come toward the van. She thought, Is there any way I can get myself out of this?

Myron came to the van and asked Dana, "You ready?"

Dana took a deep breath and said, "I'm scared. Everybody's going to be looking at me."

Myron said, "Come on, you are going to be fine."

Dana got out of the van and said, "Let's go. I can do this." She straightened out her clothes, took a deep breath, then exhaled.

They walked in, and the photographer took some pictures. They stood outside the door, and the song from the soundtrack *Book of Songs* started to play as they walked in. The female announcer said, "And now we have Mrs. Dana Frazier, the writer, executive producer, and the second director of the inspirational DVD movie called *Book of Songs*!"

Myron walked Dana in, and everyone started standing and clapping. All the actors were standing at a table in the front in the middle of the room. Dana heard her grandson yell, "Na-Na!" and her little cousin Penny yelled, "Go, cousin Dana!" She looked and she saw Tina and her husband had made it there. Dana just put her hand up and started waving to everyone.

Myron escorted Dana to the table with the other actors next to Chase. Chase pulled the chair out for Dana to sit down. The host announced one of the actors who had some songs on the soundtrack. He really surprised Dana. She had no idea that he could preach. He began to sing a couple of the songs that were in the soundtrack. Dana was so happy she had the pleasure of adding him in the project. One of the actors introduced him to Dana when she was shooting the movie.

Dana was always open to helping someone else. He was on an internet radio interview once for two hours. Dana thought he was a true blessing. She didn't know that he was very sick at one time until she heard that interview. He was paralyzed in a wheelchair; he almost died. He was at the banquet with his wife. She was the first to start clapping to the song he was singing.

Myron had some raffle drawings, and some of the guests won some great gifts. She also had a guest speaker who had a few plays out. He spoke about Dana as if she was going to be someone who will rise in the filmmaking business. As he spoke, he kept looking at one of the actors. One of the male actors got so bad that he was directing his speech to the wrong person. He yelled, "She's over there!" The guest speaker apologized to Dana as he continued to speak. He told them not to close their eyes on her. That a person who went through what she had been through and to bounce back with doing something she never did before was amazing.

After his speech, Myron spoke more about the movie and played some parts of it on a big screen. Then she began to talk about Dana and her life. They started to show some pictures of Dana and her family. One was a picture of Armani. Dana couldn't hold back her tears. As she tried to control her tears, the more they came down.

Dana was called up on stage to say her speech—the speech she never sat down to write. The speech she thought she would not get to speak without a voice. The voice she felt so compelled to give or say to the guest, the actors, and to her favorite sister Cindy and her two good friends, Myron and Lisa, for the honorary banquet.

Dana gracefully dried her eyes and walked up to the stage. She gave Myron a hug and took the mic. Dana had no idea if a sound would even come out of her mouth. She cleared her throat and spoke. She apologized that she lost her voice and sounded so terrible. She heard them all shout back it was all good. Dana continued to speak. Dana thanked all of her family and friends and actors who traveled to attend the event. Dana thanked all the actors individually for being a part of the production. As she talked about the roles they played, two of the actors playfully jumped into their character doing her speech. They all laughed. Dana thought that was what she loved about them, the laugher and fun. Dana thanked her son Zeek for making music in their studio for the soundtrack. Dana thanked her husband for all of his support and for not only playing one role but two roles. She thanked the special guest speaker and her daughter and son-in-law for being there for her. She spoke about her new project and some of the possible actors that she planned on giving them that opportunity to explored their talent. She thanked her sisters and her friends and all of North Carolina for their acknowledgment and the love they had shown her toward the movie.

Dana took a deep swallow to moisten her throat and said, "Most of all, I'd like to thank God for giving me the strength to stop mourning and start growing." Then as she could no longer get anything out of her dry, scratchy throat, she handed the mic over to Myron.

Myron did something that surprised Dana and all the actors. She called the actors up one by one and spoke about their role in the movie. She presented them all with a nice big trophy with their full names and the title of the movie. As she called them up one by one, Cindy was there to greet them with a hug and hand them their award, and then pose with them for a picture.

It was a beautiful event. They ate and continued to take pictures, socialize, dance, and had fun. Dana exhaled and was so relieved it was all over. She had a good drink, and so did everyone else. Acee maybe had a little too much that she got on the stage with the DJ and fell flat on her butt.

Dana and Cindy helped her up as they laugh at her. Acee, Carol, and Cindy spoke to Dana about how proud they were of Dana's success of the movie. Dana told them that she was glad Acee and Carol came to the event. Cindy and Acee were upset that all of their sisters didn't show up. Trudy and her older daughter Clare had purchased tickets but couldn't make it. It turned out that Clare had lymphedema in her leg and couldn't drive. Loren didn't make it either. Dana said that was okay that they didn't make it. All she knew was that they told her how proud they were of her.

Dana was so happy for the all actors who did appear, how they told her they felt like royalty and were treated as if they were on the red carpet. Dana told her three sisters who were there with her that she wished their mother was there with them. How upset she was that her mother didn't live long enough to see the movie.

They all hugged and shed some tears.

CPSIA information can be obtained
at www.ICGtesting.com
Printed in the USA
BVHW070723150621
609528BV00002B/333